TUSKEGEE

───── *in* ─────

PHILADELPHIA

Rising to the Challenge

ROBERT J. KODOSKY

THE
History
PRESS

Published by The History Press
Charleston, SC
www.historypress.com

(*Back cover, left*) Tuskegee Airmen: They Met the Challenge. *Mural Arts Philadelphia.*

First published 2020

Manufactured in the United States

ISBN 9781467144674

Library of Congress Control Number: 2019951843

*To the men and women of Tuskegee who served their families,
their communities and their nation throughout their lives.
Their legacy endures.*

CONTENTS

Preface   7
Acknowledgements   11
Introduction: From Philadelphia to Tuskegee—
    A Dream Realized   13

1. Ladies First: The Women of Tuskegee   33
2. Learning to Fly: The Trainers of Tuskegee   51
3. The Bombers: Bringing the Fight Home   67
4. The Ground Crew beneath Their Wings:
    The Mechanics of the Tuskegee Airmen   85
5. Essential Escorts: The Fighter Pilots of Tuskegee   109
6. Necessary Medicine:
    Medical Care and Experimentation at Tuskegee   125

Bibliography   141
About the Authors   143

Preface

In the early summer of 2018, my colleague at the American Helicopter Museum and Education Center, education director Paul Kahan, informed me that the president of the Philadelphia Area Chapter of the Tuskegee Airmen, Mr. Mel Payne, wished to speak with me. Of course, I consented immediately. At the time, I assumed that Mr. Payne wanted to discuss an oral history initiative. There remained only a few living Tuskegee Airmen in the area, and it made sense to capture their reflections on their experiences during the Second World War during that conflict's seventy-fifth commemoration.

As one who writes and teaches American military history, and as one who taught African American history as a high school social studies teacher in Philadelphia, Pennsylvania, I relished the opportunity to work with the chapter. From my time in Philadelphia, I knew city residents rightfully revered the chapter's members. The men and women of Tuskegee gave of their time generously, whether at air shows, ballgames or in classrooms, and their ongoing service to the community struck me and my students as impressive.

I had never met Mel before. A successful businessman, his contributions to the Philadelphia chapter over nearly two decades are noteworthy, particularly in working to keep the Tuskegee legacy alive for our region's youth, who benefit from its inspiration. Mel's work for the chapter is tireless, especially as he possesses no personal ties to the Tuskegee Airmen.

Mel learned of the group's history from an exhibit at the Wright-Patterson Air Force Base that he encountered while on a business trip through Dayton,

Ohio. The history he saw chronicled there transformed him. Mel returned to Philadelphia, sought out the city's chapter and continues to serve it with great energy.

I looked forward to meeting Mel but did wonder about the necessity of another oral history endeavor. The Tuskegee experience, particularly in the last thirty years, received a good deal of attention from the press, historians and even Hollywood. I wondered what another history might add to the existing historical documentation. I need not have worried. I knew this within the first few moments I spent with Mel.

Mel came to my office at West Chester University, and we talked. He quickly explained that the chapter possessed plenty of oral histories—it required no more. Instead, he wanted to talk about the idea he had for a book. While many now knew of the Tuskegee Airmen and the group's experience during the Second World War, they only possessed a superficial understanding. One that privileged the pilots to the exclusion of everybody else—mechanics, nurses, administrative staff, even bombers. And of course, as Mel pointed out, almost nobody understood the role that women played in the Tuskegee experience.

The merits of Mel's proposal appeared obvious. I knew this as a teacher, observing in textbooks and other materials made for students, particularly during Black History Month. Most schools now teach the importance of the Tuskegee Airmen but do so in what I call a "fly by" fashion. The kind of book Mel suggested promised to serve as a corrective, to render the Tuskegee experience in its historical complexity.

Moreover, it contained the chance to provide deserving role models of every member, in addition to the fighter pilots. Thinking along these lines, Mel shared his hope of providing scholarships to young people tied to the various types of service that the men and women of Tuskegee performed. Mel and I quickly agreed any book we produced should serve as a means for that: to fund scholarships. All author proceeds from this work will do just that.

I became excited, especially at the prospect of bringing in some of my university's finest young historians to collaborate with me in completing the project. This provided an excellent opportunity for West Chester University history students to "do history," to help Mel and me render as better understood such an important part of our nation's past. Yet, Mel had more.

The other thing people did not understand widely, Mel explained, is that the stories of the men and women of Tuskegee did not end with the Second World War. They returned home, many to the greater Philadelphia area, only to experience the same racism they confronted prior to serving their country. Nothing changed, but they had. They possessed a new strength and the resolve to persevere. They did this and passed it along to their families and to others in the community.

Mel's observation resonated. Educators and others often present history in compartmentalized fashion. Chapters in textbooks on events such as World War II and the civil rights movement make history more manageable for teachers and students. They artificially disconnect reality, though. They do not succeed in demonstrating the frustrations experienced by African Americans who served their country despite racial oppression abroad and how that contributed to their willingness to continue serving their nation by fighting against racism at home.

So many of the men and women of Tuskegee who returned to Philadelphia dedicated their lives—not just a few years—to serving the greater good. They won many battles. This story needs telling, as all these years later, many battles remain. The Philadelphia chapter of Tuskegee Airmen offers hope that they might yet be won. I knew this immediately in meeting with the many family members who contributed to this book. They shared their memories and their pride of the legacies left by their parents and grandparents, their uncles and aunts. Tuskegee forever shaped their families. Their gratitude fills them with a powerful drive to give back. They do this with great success.

This book conveys the experiences of the men and women of Tuskegee, largely through their own words and those of their families. It calls attention to the desire of young African American men and women, seventy-five years ago, to fight for the right to serve their country. Once they secured that, they never stopped. The city of Philadelphia and the United States of America are better as a result. Grasping this history, in all its complexity, enables the men and women of Tuskegee to continue to serve us all.

Acknowledgements

T his book resulted from a community effort. It derives from the passion and service to the Tuskegee legacy exhibited always by Philadelphia chapter president Mel Payne. Mel is a Philadelphia treasure, as are the family members who generously contributed their stories, read drafts and offered suggestions along the way. These include Deborah E. Butler, Albert Brown, Leslie Cousins, Bruce Williams, Rob Williams, David Draper and Regina Powell. They, along with the entire Philadelphia chapter of Tuskegee Airmen, made this book possible.

Before meeting with this group for the first time, I had the pleasure of talking to J. Banks Smither, the editor who guided me through the proposal process and served as a champion of this work to secure publication from The History Press. Banks is the editor every author should have in one's corner. His guidance and expertise proved instrumental throughout.

So, too, did the support and encouragement I received from Dean Jen Bacon and Associate Dean Hyoejin Yoon from the College of Arts and Humanities at West Chester University. My colleagues in the history department additionally shared ideas, guidance and enthusiasm. Carole Marciano, our department administrator, provided essential help in orchestrating various meeting and managing the photos that appear in the book.

I am fortunate to work in such a dynamic department, certainly one of the very best there is. That includes alumni such as Karl Helicher, who, over many lunches, always proves encouraging and ready to help. So, too, does Lillian Morrison, the veteran center coordinator at West

Chester University. Her work on behalf of veterans on campus and in the community routinely inspires.

The mural produced by artist Martin Akinlana for the Philadelphia Mural Arts program, *Tuskegee Airmen: They Met the Challenge*, constitutes a fitting tribute to the Tuskegee Airmen. The work inspires all who see it in West Philadelphia by reminding them of all that is possible. Its imagery offered a useful framework in writing the introduction here.

Paul Kahan, educational director at the American Helicopter Museum and Education Center, began the whole process by introducing me to Mel. Paul is a fellow alum of Temple University, a terrific historian, an educator— one I am proud to know. I will always be grateful that he followed through with the introduction request and then continued to offer assistance along the way, from suggesting publishers to arranging events at the museum.

West Chester University graduate student Okoteh Sackitey and alum Pete Connolly made important early contributions to this work that inform the chapters on Tuskegee's trainers and mechanics.

Finally, there are my fellow contributors. All of them are current or former students. Matthew, Michael W., Brandon, Jeffrey, Michael K. and Steven. I am glad you all are not here right now, as I would have to hide the tear in my eyes. You each make me prouder than I possess the ability to articulate appropriately. In many ways, this has been a teacher's dream project. To publish such a terrific piece of history with one's students will remain the highlight of my career. Each of you performed under pressure with a level of professionalism any historian would admire. Thank you all.

INTRODUCTION
From Philadelphia to Tuskegee– A Dream Realized

PHILADELPHIA-TUSKEGEE CONNECTION

Begun in 1994 as an anti-graffiti initiative, the Mural Arts program of Philadelphia stands as one of the nation's most extensive public art initiatives, responsible for thousands of murals across the city. It operates according to the slogan "every mural starts in the community." Each piece of art reflects this. Perhaps none more than the program's three thousandth mural, dedicated on June 14, 2009. Located at 16 South Thirty-Ninth in West Philadelphia, and featured on this book's cover, *Tuskegee Airmen: They Met the Challenge* is the creation of artist Martin Akinlana. Still, its origins and ownership reside within the surrounding community.

This is fitting. Eight of the Airmen depicted are the youthful versions of chapter members. This suggests the connection existing between Tuskegee and Philadelphia—the home for many Airmen before and after World War II. The Tuskegee Airmen, of course, hailed from all over the United States. According to Tuskegee University, anybody who served at Tuskegee Army Airfield between 1941 and 1949 constitutes a documented original Tuskegee Airman (DOTA). This comprises an estimated sixteen to nineteen thousand personnel.

Of that number, Tuskegee University officially acknowledges 996 individuals who graduated as pilots. This hints at part of the rationale behind this book. Long marginalized in histories of the Second World War, in part due to recent Hollywood films such as *Red Tails* (20th Century Fox, 2012), and the decision of the U.S. Congress and President George W. Bush to award the Tuskegee Airmen collectively with the Congressional Medal of

Honor in March 2007, the Tuskegee Airmen gained their deserved place in history and in the public imagination.

This occurred, however, with the focus of films and political officials on the program's pilots. Only a fraction served in this capacity. The bulk of individuals served as medical, mechanical and support staff. In addition to the 332rd Fighter Group and the 477th Bombardment Group, individuals served in air service groups such as the 96th and 387th, along with the 115th Army Air Forces Base Unit. The Philadelphia mural, with the input of local Tuskegee Airmen, exhibits this by featuring not only pilots but also others, such as parachute riggers and mechanics. Its representation of the Tuskegee experience stands as unique.

As does the contribution made by the greater Philadelphia area to the Tuskegee Airmen. While many imagine the Airmen exclusively as World War II African American aviators, they also assume the group's membership originated in Tuskegee, Alabama. According to Tuskegee University, not a single pilot came from the entire state of Alabama. Many, though, did come from the Philadelphia area. Thirty-six Airmen listed the city as their place of origin, with others citing Philadelphia suburbs: Ardmore (3), Bryn Mawr (2), Lincoln (1), Norristown (1) and Yeadon (1). Four more came from right across the Delaware River: Camden, New Jersey (3), and Trenton, New Jersey (1).

The total number of pilots that the Philadelphia area contributed to the Tuskegee program then, forty-eight, outnumbered those from Los Angeles, California (47), by one. It equals the combined number from Washington, D.C. (24), and the city of New York (24). Only Chicago, Illinois (66), sent more to Tuskegee to become pilots than did the Philadelphia area. At its peak membership, the Philadelphia chapter of Tuskegee Airmen consisted of sixty-five members, including Airmen, family and friends.

Philadelphia's contribution to Tuskegee reflects the Great Migration, the period between 1910 and 1930 when African Americans migrated from the southern United States to northern cities to escape Jim Crow laws and racial segregation and seek out economic opportunities. Over those twenty years, Philadelphia's African American population nearly tripled, from 85,000 to 220,000.

Besides the substantial increase Philadelphia experienced in its population of African Americans, the city developed into an aviation hub used by the military. Philadelphia occupied a key location in the national airmail system during World War I. Army officials trained reserve aviators by having them fly the mail between New York City and Washington, D.C., with a stop in

Philadelphia Tuskegee Airmen Dr. Eugene Richardson and Roscoe Draper with children at the state capitol building in Harrisburg, Pennsylvania. *Philadelphia Chapter, Tuskegee Airmen.*

Assistant Secretary of War John J. McCloy. *National Archives.*

Philadelphia. They built an airfield in northeast Philadelphia and a base in the Essington section of the city for the Second Aero Squadron.

Moreover, aviation pioneers such as Arthur Young, E. Burke Wilford, Rod and Wallace Kellett and Harold Pitcairn experimented on airfields they constructed in and around the city. Philadelphians grew accustomed to looking to the skies to spot planes, autogiros and even early helicopters prior to World War II. Philadelphia's Franklin Institute hosted the first annual Rotating Wing Aircraft meeting, sponsored by the Philadelphia chapter of the Aeronautical Sciences in 1938.

With its sizeable African American population and its concentration of aviation development, the Philadelphia area occupied a unique position to contribute to the military's increasing need for air personnel in the late 1930s. Anticipating the country's involvement in World War II, the U.S. Army needed tens of thousands of pilots, along with an even greater number of others, such as mechanics, in supporting roles. Following a model adopted by Europeans, the United States created the Civilian Pilot Training Program (CPTP) in 1938 to help the army meet its demand.

THE UNITS OF TUSKEGEE

The CPTP operated through thousands of universities and private flight schools nationwide. While it remained segregated, the CPTP did not discriminate according to race. This enabled two thousand African Americans to graduate as pilots. The Tuskegee Institute became part of the CPTP in 1940. In January 1941, the U.S. War Department designated Tuskegee as the training ground for a new "Negro Pursuit Squadron," constituted as the 99th Pursuit Squadron three months later. Eventually, the 100th, 301st and 302nd joined the 99th to compose the 332nd Fighter Group, constituted on the Fourth of July in 1942.

The 332nd Fighter Group came to be called the Red Tails. This derived from the Fighter Group pilot's decision, for easy recognition and *esprit de corps*, to paint the tails of their aircraft—initially Republic P-47 Thunderbolts and later North American P-51 Mustangs—red. Colonel Benjamin Oliver Davis commanded the 332nd. The fourth African American to graduate West Point (1936), as a captain, Davis completed the first training class at Tuskegee and became the first African American officer to solo a U.S. Army Air Corps aircraft. Davis personally led dozens of missions and earned the Silver Star, the Distinguished Flying Cross and the Legion of Merit.

The 332nd mirrored the success of its commander. First with the 12th Air Force (June 1943–May 1944) and then with the 15th (June 1944–May 1945), it flew 1,578 missions and carried out 15,533 combat sorties, achieving 112 aerial kills. In serving escort duty 179 times for the 15th, the 332nd achieved a stellar, but not perfect, record of not losing bombers. Eighty-four Tuskegee Airmen lost their lives during the Second World War, including eighty pilots. An additional thirty pilots ended up downed or captured.

The 332nd received essential support from the 96th Air Service Group, originally designated the 96th Maintenance Group and established on March 13, 1942. The 96th represented the only African American air service group to serve in a combat theater during World War II until April 1945, when the 523rd and 524th replaced it. As with the 332nd Fighter Group, the 96th first received assignment to the 12th Air Force when it arrived in Italy in January 1944, and then became reassigned to the 15th Air Force in May.

The mission of the 96th entailed providing food, shelter and medical attention to downed pilots and crews while working to service the aircraft. This involved all types of repairs, including engine replacement and salvaging aircraft that stood beyond repair. In December 1944, for example, bad weather forced several bombers to land at other airfields. The 96th responded by performing necessary service to the aircraft while caring for more than two hundred aircrew members, enabling them to access both food and shelter. The bomb crews that the 96th ably supported remained all white throughout the war.

African Americans served in the 477th Bombardment Group. This consisted of the 616th, 617th, 618th and 619th Bombardment Squadrons. Constituted on May 9, 1943, nearly a year after the 332nd, it remained stateside. The reason for this is both simple and tragic. The 477th faced obstructionist policies issued by openly racist white commanders. The 477th persevered and ultimately triumphed. With the aid of African American press, sympathetic members of Congress and the National Association for the Advancement of Colored People (NAACP), the Army Committee on Negro Troop Policy, headed by Philadelphia native John J. McCloy, intervened in support of the 477th.

In May 1945, the 477th officially became the 477th Composite Group with the addition of 99th Fighter Squadron. Colonel Davis became the group's commanding officer. According to a First Air Force inspection, the morale and the effectiveness of the group improved dramatically under its new commander. The unit received its plans to participate in the ongoing war in the Pacific against Imperial Japan.

Tuskegee Airmen Museum, Tuskegee, Alabama. *The George F. Landegger Collection of Alabama Photographs in Carol M. Highsmith's America, Library of Congress, Prints and Photographs Division.*

Philadelphia Chapter assembles for photo. *Philadelphia Chapter, Tuskegee Airmen.*

Before the 477th could deploy, however, the war came to an end. Members of the group fought their war at home rather than abroad, and they succeeded. For many Tuskegee Airmen, at times, the two fronts appeared as one and the same. Martin Akinlana's mural *Tuskegee Airmen: They Met the Challenge* reveals this.

According to the Mural Arts program's website, Akinlana "worked closely with the Philadelphia chapter of the Tuskegee Airmen," as did Mural Arts students who met with Airmen and painted their portraits. Elements of the mural's design derive from Airmen descriptions of boyhood dreams of flying. This includes the depiction of a boy playing with a toy airplane. As the rest of the mural reveals, those dreams were realized. The featured image consists of the head and goggles of an African American pilot in combat.

THE NEED FOR A "DOUBLE VICTORY"

Before they could fly over the considerable gap that separated their dreams and reality, however, Tuskegee pilots required access to planes. The racism prevalent at the time warded against this. The Philadelphia mural's viewers glimpse this through the pilot's goggles where the image appears of Charles Alfred "The Chief" Anderson Sr. A native of Bryn Mawr, Pennsylvania, a Philadelphia suburb, the Chief began his life in 1907.

As Michael J. Weiss writes in the second chapter of this book, "Learning to Fly: The Trainers of Tuskegee," early in life, Anderson "decided to be a pilot." But in his attempts to fly, his applications to various flight schools and the Pennsylvania National Guard, "the color of his skin resulted in rejection."

Largely self-taught, the Chief finally took flight in 1929. In 1940, Anderson accepted an invitation from the Tuskegee Institute in Alabama to serve as chief civilian flight instructor for the government's new program to train African American pilots, the CPTP. In that capacity Anderson earned much publicity for piloting a flight for First Lady Eleanor Roosevelt in March 1941.

By June, the United States Army named the Chief as ground commander and chief instructor for the United States' first all–African American fight squadron, the Ninety-Ninth. The Chief and his pilots, as the Philadelphia mural's title indicates, met the challenge. But they grew aware that many more challenges remained. Even as they took flight, for the sake of their nation, the gap between their dreams and reality appeared wide.

The Philadelphia mural prominently features two signs. On the viewer's left reads "No Colored Allowed," while on the right, "Whites Only." In learning to fly, Tuskegee Airmen first had to hurdle the numerous barriers that others placed before them. The stories relayed in this book render that evident. For example, in chapter 3, "The Bombers," Michael Kowalski chronicles the struggles that Bert Levy and James Williams endured attempting to enlist in the United States Army's Air Corps.

While Levy and Williams ultimately succeeded, they and their colleagues in the 477th Air Bombardment Group found the army less than welcoming. This included U.S. Army general Henry "Hap" Arnold, head of the army air forces. As Kowalski observes, Arnold used his position to "try to end the initiative to enable blacks to serve as bombers before it could get started." This pushed the 477th's activation date back to January 15, 1944. Throughout, members of the unit endured segregated facilities, shortages of equipment and the refusal of promotion. All this while pledging their lives to fight against the United States' enemies, including racist Nazi Germany and Imperial Japan.

As Brandon Langston shows in chapter 5, "Essential Escorts: The Fighter Pilots of Tuskegee," a 1925 report issued by the U.S. Army War College in Carlisle, Pennsylvania, shaped the way army officials thought about African Americans in uniform. It observed that the brains of African Americans averaged ten ounces smaller than those of whites. It further advised that "the negro is a rank coward in the dark."

This contributed to the widespread embrace by African Americans, both military and civilian, of the "Double V" campaign initiated by the *Pittsburgh Courier* in 1942. Unlike during the First World War, when African Americans responded to President Woodrow Wilson's call to "make the world safe for democracy" and returned to continued segregation and racism at home, "Double V" pressed African Americans to fight against oppression abroad and stateside to achieve a double victory.

A struggle for equality proved necessary on military bases and off. Especially if arriving from one of the United States' less overtly racist areas, Tuskegee Airmen often first encountered the harsh reality of racism on the train ride to training camps down south. In crossing the Mason Dixon line, the traditional demarcation between the northern and southern states, personnel required blacks to move to the front of the train.

This was intended to make African American passengers choose between two unsavory options. They could swelter in the heat with windows closed or breath the smoke and cinders pouring out of the train's engine. Once they arrived at their designated training camps, Tuskegee Airmen often found surrounding communities to be as uncomfortable as their travel.

As testimonies from various chapters in the book demonstrate, Tuskegee Airmen who deployed to Italy found the inhabitants of that country more hospitable than those they encountered in Fort Knox, Kentucky; Biloxi, Mississippi; Tuskegee, Alabama; and Detroit, Michigan. In fact, whites in Tuskegee sought to thwart the very construction of an airbase and lobbied against African American military police carrying guns. In Detroit, a northern city, race riots provided the backdrop for black officers stationed at Selfridge Field who found their access to the officer's club prohibited.

Wherever they trained, Tuskegee Airmen often became near prisoners on base—restricted in the surrounding communities by curfews and refusal of service, including from public libraries. Such treatment extended even to Washington, D.C. Pilot James Williams, as Michael Kowalski chronicles in chapter 3, "Bombers," once flew a white officer from Tuskegee to D.C. Williams flew back to Tuskegee directly after he dropped the colonel off at his destination. Because of his race, Williams "was not allowed to stay at any of the hotels."

There did exist occasional efforts to bridge, even if temporarily, the gap between the Tuskegee Airmen's dreams and their reality. Kowalski writes of another instance experienced by Williams, one that involved transporting an interracial group of airmen from one base to another. As the African Americans attempted to board a bus behind their white comrades, the driver instructed that he "would not be accepting any black passengers."

The white pilots stepped out of the bus. They informed the driver that "he would be driving all of them or none of them." The driver relented. A new reality appeared within reach, if even for a moment, as the gap separating dreams from reality for African Americans narrowed.

Racist incidents continued to transpire, and these did not only impact Tuskegee pilots. They affected the thousands of other Tuskegee Airmen who remained on the ground. Jeffrey Markland reveals this in chapter 4, "The Ground Crew beneath Their Wings: The Mechanics of the Tuskegee Airmen." Tuskegee Airman mechanic Carey Lee McRae Sr.'s daughter Jacqui recalls the stories her father told her.

One of these conveyed the humiliation of officials moving McRae to offer a better seat to a German prisoner of war. Imagine. An American citizen pledged to defend his nation against a racist enemy regime moved by his superior to enable the enemy greater comfort. Another memory of

Eastern regional meeting 2005. *Philadelphia Chapter, Tuskegee Airmen.*

McRae's, even worse, involved the lynching of an African American officer at Keesler Air Force Base in Biloxi, Mississippi.

One of McRae's fellow Tuskegee Airman mechanics, Henry Lincoln Moore, nearly refused to return stateside after his deployment to Italy. Moore found the freedom and equality there, during war, that he found lacking in the United States. Only the Servicemen's Readjustment Act of 1944, or the GI Bill, with the opportunities it provided for veterans to receive a higher education, convinced Moore otherwise. He returned home at war's end, possessing seven battle stars and campaign medals.

THE WOMEN OF TUSKEGEE

While the men of Tuskegee faced racism, for the women of Tuskegee, there existed the additional problem of sexism. The very name Airmen, of course, resists gender inclusiveness. Tuskegee women earned little recognition for their service. That largely remains the case. For example, as of August 2019, the popular online encyclopedia Wikipedia makes no mention at all of women in its lengthy entry about the Tuskegee Airmen.

Tuskegee University's website dedicated to the Tuskegee experience cites the eligibility requirements for documented official Tuskegee Airmen to include "Anyone—man or woman" who participated in any facet of the "Tuskegee Experience." While the website contains a great deal of information, including the name of every pilot who graduated from Tuskegee, it contains no detailed information about Tuskegee's women.

Yet at least two hundred of Tuskegee's Airmen owe their wings to a woman. They learned how to fly from Willa Brown, a Chicago native who began flying in the 1930s. She opened the Coffey School of Aeronautics, which participated in the government's CPTP, with her husband, Cornelius.

At Tuskegee, Philadelphia's "Chief" Anderson, Tuskegee's head flight instructor, took Mildred Hemmons under his wings. Under Anderson's tutelage, Carter earned her private pilot's license in 1941. She married Tuskegee Airman Herman Carter a year later, following his appointment as a lieutenant. While Lieutenant Carter went off to war as a fighter pilot, his new bride remained grounded.

At that time, her gender prevented her from flying military planes. The army air corps, however, made Mildred Carter its first civilian hire. Like some of the other women who ventured to serve at Tuskegee, Carter adopted a dual role. She provided support to both the program and her husband.

While she worked at a variety of tasks at Tuskegee—from administrative work to clearing airfields—Carter applied to the Women's Air Force Service Pilot (WASP) program. Created in August 1943, the WASP program used civilian female pilots to ferry and test planes, so male pilots would be free for combat duty. Though she was qualified for the program, it rejected Carter because of her race. She spent the rest of the war at the base in Tuskegee, performing her duties on the ground, which included rigging parachutes.

The Philadelphia mural *Tuskegee Airmen: They Met the Challenge* features female representation, including parachute riggers. This represents the participation of those women from Philadelphia who served to support the Airmen, including Callie O. Gentry. Her story is chronicled by Steven J. Zaharick in chapter 1, "Ladies First: The Women of Tuskegee."

As a stenographer, Gentry supported the 477th Composite Group for about a year. This included, on one occasion, taking depositions from witnesses at a crash site, which filled two shorthand books. Unaccustomed to segregation growing up in Philadelphia, Gentry recalls that what she experienced in the military constituted "whatever you've read…and then some."

And then some indeed. As with their male counterparts, the women of Tuskegee followed their dreams of service and equality. They almost immediately confronted the chasm in their way—one forged by racism. A native of Harlem, New York, Irma "Pete" Dryden boarded a train in April 1943, heading to Tuskegee where she volunteered to lend her skills as a nurse. She and two other African American nurses learned that they would transfer to a segregated train in the nation's capital, Washington, D.C.

Once aboard the new train, they received strict orders about dining. They could only take their meals at certain times in the dining car, behind a closed curtain to avoid upsetting white passengers. Years later, Dryden confessed to CNN that she "had never been exposed to something so humiliating." And like many of her contemporaries who experienced such indignities within the country they defended, Dryden proved resilient and grew stronger.

This certainly proved the case for Miss Alma Elizabeth Bailey who served as one of Tuskegee's nurses. At least forty-one women worked as nurses at Tuskegee, but this number, like the number of women overall who participated in the program, remains an estimate. As recently as 2014, Amelia Jones, who served for two years in the Ninety-Ninth Pursuit Squadron under Colonel Benjamin O. Davis, received the prestigious Tuskegee red jacket to commemorate her service.

As the National Park Service reported, this only happened by chance. The former sergeant Jones revealed her story to a few fellow participants dressed in Tuskegee Airmen uniforms during Honor Flight Savannah, a visit of veterans to the National Mall. One of the Mall's interpreters, John McCaskill, engaged Jones in conversation about her service and worked to assist her in gaining the long-overdue public recognition that her wartime service deserved.

Miss Alma Bailey's wartime experience did not include any time at Tuskegee Airfield. Instead, Miss Bailey worked at the John A. Anderson Memorial Hospital, established in 1892 as the Tuskegee Institute Hospital and Nurse Training School. As Matthew Rothfuss notes in chapter 6, "Necessary Medicine: Medical Care and Experimentation at Tuskegee," by the Second World War the hospital gained recognition as "the best hospital for black patients in Alabama." Yet, as Rothfuss chronicles, it also housed something sinister.

Miss Bailey received assignment to the hospital's ward that served as the site for the Tuskegee Study of Untreated Syphilis in the African American, a forty-year initiative of the U.S. Public Health Service. This sought to monitor the progress of syphilis in untreated patients even after 1947, when

Nurses of Tuskegee. *Philadelphia Chapter, Tuskegee Airmen.*

penicillin became the standard treatment. It involved hundreds of infected African American men and hundreds more who served as a control group, leading to the infection of spouses and newborns.

The study remained a secret until 1972, but Miss Alma Bailey encountered it directly in 1943. Rothfuss explains the horrors Miss Bailey endured, not knowing the patients constituted a grand experiment even as she worried of contracting the disease herself. Miss Bailey only learned the truth about the program when a whistle-blower leaked its details decades later. While the racist nature of the program remained hidden from Miss Bailey at the time, the racism prevalent in Tuskegee proved overt.

While downtown Tuskegee was just a short walk for Miss Bailey from her dormitory, it might as well have been a hundred miles away. For Miss Bailey and the other African American nurses, Tuskegee remained inaccessible. They could only venture into town in large groups during daylight hours. Officials discouraged even that, though. Instead, they steered the nurses to stores temporarily constructed directly off campus grounds. Visiting these also mandated a chaperone.

The racism that Miss Bailey confronted was almost constant. The sexism, equally as threatening, manifested suddenly in the most unexpected of places. For the chance to serve Tuskegee Airmen, Miss Bailey assumed additional duties at the local veterans' hospital. There she cared for Airmen assigned to the psychiatric ward. Back from the war, they suffered from a range of symptoms now recognized as post-traumatic stress disorder (PTSD). Treatment remained primitive. It involved electrical shock.

Often alone in the ward with dozens of men who were damaged emotionally and mentally by war, Miss Bailey and her fellow nurses were susceptible to physical assault and rape. As Rothfuss discusses in chapter 6, guards expected favorable treatment from nurses in exchange for providing the protection expected of them. As Miss Bailey refused to "date" any of the guards, they left her unwatched. This led to assault and attempted rape, which Miss Bailey miraculously thwarted. Other nurses did not also prove so fortunate.

Despite the incident, as Rothfuss notes, when interviewed about her service, Miss Bailey "wears her Tuskegee Airmen baseball cap proudly." This emerged as the case for many of the women and men who worked to narrow the gaps that sexism and racism placed between their dreams and reality. As Tuskegee nurse Irma Dryden shared with CNN, ordered to eat separate from white passengers and behind a curtain, this enabled her to realize that she "can overcome anything" and can help whomever she encountered.

WAR OVER, FIGHT CONTINUES

Of course, racism and sexism hardly proved vanquished by victory in the Second World War. This frustration led some to renounce their service and experience a profound sense of disillusionment. For example, Jeffrey Markland writes in chapter 4 that, according to his daughter Jacqui, Carey Lee McCrae Sr. dropped out of high school to enlist. He wanted to prove the capability of African Americans to serve the country they loved. He did so admirably as a Tuskegee mechanic, providing essential support to the 332nd Fighting Group in Italy.

After the war, McCrae was honorably discharged and returned to Philadelphia with many medals. Still, he could not get a job. His skin color prevented this, as garage owners openly informed the wartime mechanic. It proved too much. According to his daughter, McCrae incinerated his uniform and his medals. He grew full of "deep bitterness and resentment" and refused to acknowledge his service as a Tuskegee Airman for fifty years. Jacqui grew up fully unaware of her father's wartime service. The City of Philadelphia finally recognized his service by honoring McCrae in 2000.

Like McCrae, others who served with Tuskegee learned that while they helped end one war, there existed another that reengaged them. They only achieved a single victory—the "Double V" campaign remained unfinished. Their work narrowed the gap between dream and reality, but despite their extraordinary service, it failed to close entirely. President Harry S. Truman issued Executive Order 9981 in 1948. This ended race-based discrimination in the military and led to the end of racial segregation in the United States' armed services. Discrimination and segregation remained, however, nearly everywhere else in the country.

G. Naomi Funderburg, the wife of missing-in-action Tuskegee fighter pilot Frederick Funderburg, often traveled across the country after the war to visit family members. Her son remembers one of those trips that they took together in the 1960s two decades following the Second World War's conclusion. At a stop along their way, a restaurant in Texas refused to serve them.

Despite their status as a Gold Star family —a distinction created by Woodrow Wilson in 1918 to recognize those whose loved ones failed to return from war—only skin color mattered in too many places when it came to serving G. Naomi and her son. Her son recalls that his mom wrote it off as ignorance and simply drove on. The sacrifices of Tuskegee continued. None of the Tuskegee pilots who did come home received the opportunity to fly commercially.

The two signs situated near center on *Tuskegee Airmen: They Met the Challenge*, reading "No Colored Allowed" and "Whites Only," had somehow remained in place throughout the South. The war did them no damage. In the North, there existed no signs, at least posted. Racism and segregation simply persisted as it did before the war, systematically.

New housing developers, such as William J. Levitt, the architect of postwar suburbia who constructed Levittowns on the outskirts of New York City and Philadelphia, refused to sell homes to African Americans. Military veterans purchased many of these homes using money from the G.I. Bill. For Tuskegee Airmen, this was not an option. Their choices for housing remained limited, confined to neighborhoods that accepted African American residents and demeaned their service to their country.

In the areas where they could purchase homes—areas vacated by whites for the suburbs, such as North Philadelphia—African Americans struggled against the practice of redlining. In the 1930s, Home Owners' Loan Corporation produced maps that identified "undesirable" neighborhoods by color coding them.

Roscoe Draper (*second from right*) and fellow members of Black Pilot Association of Philadelphia. *Philadelphia Chapter, Tuskegee Airmen.*

While white Anglo-Saxon Protestant areas earned the most desirable color, green, African American neighborhoods uniformly received the mark of red, meaning hazardous. This practice remained legal until 1968 and meant that while African Americans were locked out of white neighborhoods, securing a loan and insurance for home ownership in a redlined area proved very expensive.

And yet, they all kept working, resuming their fight on different fronts at home, within the country they defended. This sometimes also included the neighborhoods where they and their families resided. After the war, James Williams, a Tuskegee bomber, became one of the first African Americans to graduate from Muhlenburg College in Allentown, Pennsylvania. He then attended medical school and became the director of pathology at Mercy-Douglass Hospital, a historically black health care facility located in West Philadelphia. This failed to impress some of his white neighbors in his racially integrated neighborhood.

As Michael Kowalski recounts in chapter 3, one of his neighbors, while apparently intoxicated, stood on Williams' lawn one night yelling racial slurs. Williams responded with both dignity and humor to ease the fear of his children, who witnessed the incident. Williams informed his family of his intention to get a large German shepherd and name it with the slurs used by his neighbors. Williams reasoned then that if the neighbor came back and opened his mouth in hatred, the dog would charge to him in response.

They Met the Challenge Again and Again

The mural created by Martin Akinlana for the Philadelphia Mural Arts program is titled *The Tuskegee Airmen: They Met the Challenge*. It is a terrific title, but perhaps it should be pluralized. The men and women of Tuskegee, as evidenced by those from Philadelphia, met many challenges stemming from both racism and sexism, at home and abroad, before, during and after the war. And still, they thrived, often in ways that reflected their ongoing willingness to serve their communities and their nation.

As an African American physician, Dr. James Williams provided great comfort to his patients. In a segregated health care system tainted by the experimentation conducted at Tuskegee, Dr. Williams proved one to trust. He also returned to serve his nation. He joined the air force reserve and worked as a primary care physician at the U.S. Air Force Base in Dover, Delaware. When discharged a second time in 1973, Dr. Williams had earned the rank of lieutenant colonel.

At his passing in 2017, Dr. Williams once more took flight as a Lonely Eagle. The press dubbed the cadets at Tuskegee as "Lonely Eagles," and the label endures. Tuskegee Airmen use it to identify their dead. The ceremony held for Lonely Eagles seeks to celebrate their legacy and honor their heroism. The national Tuskegee Airmen Incorporated commemorates Lonely Eagles at its annual convention with a table of honor that features a folded American flag and a candle. The single flame is symbolic of the determination and spirit of the Tuskegee Airmen that burns eternal.

In becoming a Lonely Eagle, Dr. Williams joined twelve others from the Philadelphia chapter of Tuskegee Airmen. These include C. Alfred "The Chief" Anderson, Richard S.A. Armistead, Reverend Henry H. Baldwin, Benjamin L. Calloway, William M. Cousins, Fredrick D. Funderburg (MIA-shot down), John L. Harrison Jr., Walter P. Manning (MIA-shot down), Henry L. Moore, Pierce T. Ramsey, Edward Smith and Luther H. Smith (returned POW).

The Lonely Eagle ceremony constitutes a fitting tribute to its members and serves to celebrate the group's remarkable legacy. Philadelphia Lonely Eagle John L. Harrison Jr., for example, saw combat as a fighter pilot during the Second World War and then continued to fly for the air force for another two decades. By the time he retired with the rank of major, Harrison had crossed the Pacific Ocean fifty times and the Atlantic thirty times. He retired from the military in 1963, but his career of service continued unabated. Harrison's civilian achievements proved as notable as those from his time in the military.

Harrison went on to become an officer and a director for the Peace Corps, based in East Africa. He worked in the administrations of President Richard M. Nixon and Pennsylvania governor Dick Thornburgh. Back in Philadelphia, Harrison became the director of affirmative action for the Boeing Aircraft Company. When he became a Lonely Eagle in 2017, he had reached the age of ninety-six. His family included four children, nine grandchildren and six great-grandchildren.

A fellow Lonely Eagle from the Philadelphia chapter, also a former fighter pilot, William M. Cousins waged his second war—a battle against racist housing policies, such as redlining. He first worked on fair housing for the City of Philadelphia. In 1961, Cousins took a job with the State of Pennsylvania that afforded him the opportunity to administer his state's first fair housing law. Cousins left his job with the state in 1965 to work for the federal Housing and Finance Agency, the predecessor to the Department of Housing and Urban Development. He became a Lonely Eagle in 2014 at the age of ninety.

Lonely Eagle Henry L. Moore only came back to Philadelphia because of the G.I. Bill. His time in Italy largely convinced him to leave the racist America behind. When he did return, Moore made the most of it. He became a scientist and worked in a variety of capacities, including as the engineering supervisor for the U.S. Army Metrology and Calibration Center. He further worked to educate and inspire the youth of Philadelphia. Moore taught math and science, first at Roosevelt Middle School and then at Abraham Lincoln High School in Philadelphia. Moore kept much of his distinguished World War II service quiet, even with his family. Moore became a Lonely Eagle in 2012.

The legacy of Philadelphia's Lonely Eagles resonates powerfully both locally and nationally. During the war, Luther H. Smith flew more than 130 missions as a Tuskegee fighter pilot. In both aerial combat and ground strafing missions, Luther destroyed twelve enemy aircraft. For his service, Smith

Philadelphia's Young Eagles. *Philadelphia Chapter, Tuskegee Airmen.*

received the Distinguished Flying Cross, an Air Medal with six Oak Leaf Clusters, the Purple Heart and eight European and Mediterranean Theater Campaign Ribbons. He also earned the Prisoner of War Medal. The engine of Smith's P-51 Mustang caught fire on Friday the thirteenth of October 1944. German soldiers pulled his broken body from a tree in Yugoslavia.

Smith's captors regularly questioned him about his willingness to serve a country that lynched African Americans. By all accounts, Smith remained defiant. He consistently underscored his pride in serving until the day he regained his freedom in May 1945. At that time, he weighed only seventy pounds. Smith spent the next two years receiving treatment in military hospitals before receiving his discharge at the rank of captain.

Once back home, Smith earned his bachelor's degree in mechanical engineering from the University of Iowa. He began his career with General Electric in Schenectady, New York, and transferred to the company's aerospace division in Philadelphia in the late 1950s. He worked there until his retirement in 1988, earning two U.S. patents. Smith published numerous technical documents and publications and worked on special assignments with the U.S. Air Force, the National Aeronautics and Space Administration (NASA) and the U.S. Navy Submarine Command. Smith's efforts earned him the Society of Automotive Engineers, Aerospace International, Franklin W. Kolk Aerospace Industry Award.

Locally, Smith served on the boards of Delaware County Community College and the Radnor Township School District. He regularly spoke to school groups about his Second World War experience and proved instrumental in helping the Pennsylvania Veterans Museum produce the documentary film *On Freedom's Wings: Bound for Glory, the Legacy of the Tuskegee Airmen*. In 2006, Smith was inducted into the Iowa Aviation Hall of Fame while also earning the University of Iowa's Distinguished Award for Alumni Achievement. According to the University of Iowa's School of Engineering website, Smith "contributed significantly to the achievement of racial equality in the U.S. and the world and helped change the face of the U.S. military in a remarkably short period of time."

While those words attest to Smith's remarkable life, they also capture the overall contributions of the thousands of men and women who served their nation as part of Tuskegee. Members of the Philadelphia chapter exemplify this. They fought for their nation but first had to fight for their ability to do so. They met those challenges admirably before and during the war. When they returned to the United States, the men and women of Tuskegee discovered that challenges remained. Without complaint, they rolled up their sleeves and met those too. Seventy-five years removed from the Second World War's conclusion, the men and women of Tuskegee continue to inspire. Their legacy remains vital.

1

LADIES FIRST
The Women of Tuskegee

By Steven James Zaharick II

G. NAOMI: GOLD STAR OF TUSKEGEE

Though often overlooked, women played a part in the history of Tuskegee. The pilots receive most of the attention, but women paved a path through barriers of sexism and segregation. Women encountered Tuskegee by journeying various avenues. Through marriage and service, the town and university became a part of their lives. Gertrude Naomi Funderburg and Callie Gentry were women of Tuskegee and continued the work of the group throughout their lives. The Philadelphia chapter of the Tuskegee Airmen brought these women together and allowed for the expression of their unique involvement with the group. Their impact on the Philadelphia chapter continues today.

Gertrude Naomi Funderburg, née Bowman, grew up in Philadelphia during the 1930s. She lived a simple life and learned values that would guide her. G. Naomi, as she soon came to be called, was a middle child in a family of six children. She shared a close bond with her father, Lester Bowman, who worked for Pullman Railroad and got hurt in a rail accident. Her father remained at home because of the accident, which allowed him to play a close role in the lives of his children. He helped shape G. Naomi and taught her valuable lessons. Her mother, Alice Bowman, helped keep the family afloat with cleaning jobs.

G. Naomi's son Frederick remembers his mom talking about the difficulties poor eyesight caused for her as a youth, including ridicule from her classmates. She emphasized that this did not hold her back. G. Naomi found her confidence by learning to play the piano and by earning good

Off to war, ladies first. *Library of Congress.*

grades in school. G. Naomi decided to go into the world of education. She earned a scholarship to Cheyney University, a prominent black college in Delaware County. There she learned the skills she needed to educate others. After graduating, G. Naomi sought fellowships in education. By chance, a fellowship brought her to Tuskegee, Alabama, to teach in a local school. This is when her lifelong association with Tuskegee began.

The African American community and social life in Tuskegee centered on the university and the army airbase. G. Naomi came into contact with pilots because many of her teacher friends dated men from the air base, and group dates were the norm. At first, G. Naomi had no interest in dating anyone and was content doing her work. Eventually, though, her friends brought back a young pilot named Frederick Funderburg Jr. G. Naomi hit it off with the young pilot, and the two formed a relationship. As a romantic gesture and to show off for their girls, many of the pilots would "buzz" the teachers' quarters where their girlfriends lived. This entailed flying as low to the ground as possible to generate a buzz that reverberated loudly with all below. G. Naomi could always tell which plane was Frederick because he never buzzed the quarters but would remain high in the air, doing acrobatics like a bird. Tuskegee brought together this girl from Philadelphia and boy from Monticello, Georgia.

The two soon got married, and Frederick finished his training. Before getting shipped overseas, Frederick and G. Naomi traveled around the country because of Frederick's assignments to various air bases. They enjoyed their time together, attending big band dances and many dinners. In 1944, they had their only child together, Frederick Funderburg III. It was a very happy time for the young couple, but the war loomed, and Frederick was shipped to Europe to fight the German Luftwaffe with the rest of the Tuskegee pilots.

In Europe Frederick flew the P-51 mustang *Stinky III* because G. Naomi had a difficult time changing diapers, and Frederick wanted to give a humorous nod to his wife back home. He was successful and represented his country well. In December 1944, while flying a mission over Germany, Frederick's group got hit with intense flak, and while he tried to lead his unit to safety, the unit lost track of Frederick's plane. His voice continued to make contact through the radios, but eventually, his fellow pilots heard no word from him. Frederick Funderburg Jr. went missing over Germany and never returned home.

The loss of her husband affected G. Naomi for the rest of her life. She struggled as a single mother raising her young son, but her extensive family helped her every step of the way. G. Naomi moved back to Philadelphia with her son and worked as a schoolteacher. Her parents and trips to Monticello, Georgia, to visit Frederick's parents gave G. Naomi reprieve from the loss of her husband and helped her cope. The summers in Monticello with her husband's parents provided a great environment for her son to grow up and for G. Naomi to keep her husband's memory alive. Long talks on the veranda with her mother-in-law became the bedrock of those summers in Georgia. Furthermore, her husband linked her to Tuskegee, and historians occasionally approached her for information and pictures after the war. She continued to stay in contact with men who knew Frederick from Tuskegee, and they helped her understand what happened to her husband.

G. Naomi continued her career by working at a special needs school on Spring Garden Street in Philadelphia. She worked with special needs because of her own experience of being teased and laughed at for her eyesight issues. Clearly, G. Naomi wanted to help kids get through their own tough childhoods, and her own experiences gave her great sympathy for them. She remained active in the school district and gained a position as a science collaborator. The science collaborator position held great influence in the school district. Working for the board of education, G. Naomi traveled around the school district to emphasize science projects in the school curriculum. Her career yet again took her away from Philadelphia, and she went to Arizona State University to get her master's degree.

Throughout her life, G. Naomi faced racism. She took an approach of ignoring it because she believed racism stemmed from ignorance. She did not let racism stop her from furthering her education and remaining close to family members. Her son recalls a story when he and his mother traveled across the country to visit family members in the mid-1960s. In Texas, they stopped to get food at a restaurant, and the owners turned them away, saying, "We don't serve you." Unfortunately, G. Naomi and her son were familiar with racism from their time visiting family members in Georgia and saw it as a fact of life. But her values and beliefs allowed G. Naomi to stand taller than racism, and she did not let it hurt her. The ethics that her father taught her in the 1930s filtered down to her son.

Along with her family, her faith and her church provided a safe haven and a place to seek help. G. Naomi taught at the Sunday school and often sought advice from her minister. She liked to bury herself in institutions and become part of something bigger than herself, and James Memorial United Methodist Church on Haines Street provided exactly what she needed. Tuskegee factored into G. Naomi's life here. Some of her friends and associates at church had connections to Tuskegee. Stories were swapped and relationships were built among the members associated with Tuskegee.

By the 1970s, the Philadelphia chapter of the Tuskegee Airmen was beginning to take shape, and G. Naomi found out about the group through friends in her church. Word of mouth and an article in the newspaper gathered members to the group. Because of her husband, she was able to join the group. The group sought to bring together all members of Tuskegee in the Philadelphia area. Educated men and women—doctors, educators and businesspeople—formed the group. It held a lot of talent to face any problems the Philadelphia chapter may encounter.

G. Naomi entered the group at the very beginning, and for the remainder of her life, she worked hand in hand with the Tuskegee Philadelphia chapter. In the early days, the group met in unofficial locations about once a month to plan events and benefits and to discuss the mission. G. Naomi took part in committees to organize fundraising events. One of

G. Naomi (seated, front) with Philadelphia Tuskegee Airmen. *Philadelphia Chapter, Tuskegee Airmen.*

the primary missions of the Philadelphia chapter involved scholarships for young African Americans in the community, and G. Naomi helped put together fundraisers, such as luncheons. She was industrious and humble in her work with the group. Her efforts proved tireless, and these became essential to the chapter's success.

"No man stands on his own," as G. Naomi told her son. This drove her life and pursuit of institutions. Her husband, Frederick, put her on this path, and she courageously followed it. She remained dedicated to the group until she passed away in 2016. G. Naomi's son, Frederick Funderburg III, carries on his mother's legacy and ethics.

G. Naomi experienced Tuskegee as a spouse of a pilot who never returned from combat. Her link through family allowed her to enter the group as an equal. As detailed next, Callie Gentry first encountered Tuskegee veterans while serving in the military in the 1940s. She never went to Tuskegee, but her association with the group began early in her life, much like G. Naomi.

Callie Gentry: From Philadelphia to the Women's Army Corps

Callie Gentry, née Odom, was born in South Carolina and spent the early years of her childhood in a little town called Blackville. Her mother started a job in New York City, which led the family to move to the Northeast. When Callie was five and half, her grandmother moved with her and her three sisters to live with their uncle in Philadelphia. During the Great War, her grandmother lost a son and wanted to be closer to remaining family. Callie grew up in a neighborhood surrounded by different cultures. The Quakers dominated the neighborhood and provided a safe environment.

Even during the Great Depression, Callie enjoyed a decent life. Playgrounds, schools and afterschool activities provided recreation for the kids in the neighborhood. Callie fondly remembers playing basketball as a kid. To this day, she remembers shooting a basketball across the court and scoring a basket.

This quaint lifestyle in Philadelphia allowed Callie to avoid the harshness of racism and the culture divide that existed in other parts of the country in the 1930s. The Quakers welcomed everyone to their neighborhood and treated everyone with respect and dignity. The schools were not segregated, the families watched one another's children and a closeness of community existed between all types of people. Everybody knew everybody. People from as far as Czechoslovakia and other eastern European countries lived in the same neighborhood. Callie remembers the immigrants with their babushkas and the many languages spoken in the neighborhood. Diversity was a key characteristic of Callie's childhood. The "guild house," as the locals called the Quaker Institution, was the center of life and helped create the umbrella of protection. The Quakers sheltered the neighborhood. Callie never knew what segregation was until she joined the military.

Callie went into the military in 1945. She needed to get from Philadelphia to Des Moines, Iowa. Her route took her on a train to Washington, D.C., where she hopped on the B & O Line. From the line between Philadelphia and Washington, D.C., Callie and other African Americans could sit in the same cars as whites and enjoy the comforts of traveling on a train. When she arrived in Washington, everything changed.

The African Americans on board had to move from their comfortable seats to a car behind the locomotive. The seats provided little comfort, and the lack of circulating air required the windows to be open. The black smoke from the locomotive seeped into the car and created a filthy, disgusting environment. The experience was raw and dehumanizing.

When Callie arrived in Des Moines with the other recruits, the military split them up into two groups: whites and blacks. Everyone loaded onto different trucks and headed for the destination. The trip from Washington to Des Moines gave Callie a glimpse into what kind of racial segregation existed in the country and what she could expect being in the army. Callie felt puzzled and confused on why the whites and blacks were separated because her childhood taught her that everyone was equal. Callie's tight-knit community was all she ever knew, and she experienced culture shock in her own country.

Eventually, Callie ended up at Fort Sam Houston in San Antonio, Texas. She was part of the Women's Army Corps (WAC), an auxiliary unit to the Women's Army Auxiliary Corps (WAAC), created on May 15, 1942. The program, designed to employ women to compensate for the shortage of men who were engaged in the fighting, helped the military with supply lines, clerical work and medical business. From the onset, it proved racially inclusive. This was largely a result of the efforts of educator and civil rights activist Mary McLeod Bethune, who successfully lobbied her friend First Lady Eleanor Roosevelt to enable black female participation in the war.

The WAC initiative offered unprecedented opportunities for African American women. Its unit, the 6888th Central Postal Directory Battalion, known as "Six Triple Eight," enabled the military to clear a two-year backlog of mail for Americans stationed in Europe. From February 1945 until March 1946, the unit's 855 African American women distributed mail that had accumulated in warehouses located in England and France. The unit represented the largest contingent of African American women ever to serve overseas.

The Six Triple Eight fell under the command of Major Charity Adams, the first commissioned African American WAC. By the end of the war, Lieutenant Colonel Adams was the highest-ranking African American woman in the military. Harriet West Waddy also achieved the rank of lieutenant colonel in 1948. Serving with McLeod Bethune on the Bureau of Negro Affairs, Lieutenant Colonel Waddy became an aide on WAC race relations to the program's director, Colonel Oveta Culp Hobby.

In becoming a WAC, Callie Gentry joined a progressive unit, one in which African American women made considerable strides within the existent racist and sexist culture. An officer once threatened Adams that he would replace her with a white lieutenant. The matter dropped after Adams began to file charges. In Callie's case, her training focused on being a clerk and typist. By December 1945, the United States and the Allies

Mary McLeod Bethune and First Lady Eleanor Roosevelt at the opening of the residence for African American women employed by the government. *National Archives.*

Major Charity Adams inspecting the Six Triple Eight. *National Archives.*

defeated the Axis powers, and the rebuilding process of Europe and Japan began in earnest.

Callie and the other women in her unit were slated to begin deployment in Europe to help with the occupation. The military intended for the group to help distribute mail to the servicemen throughout Europe. Callie's group consisted of white and black women. Trucks came and picked up the women for their duties. Slowly, the group dwindled as women were given their orders and the barracks emptied—all except for Callie.

On a beautiful December day in San Antonio, a noncommissioned officer visited Callie and told her that she was wanted at headquarters. This came as a shock to Callie. Why would she be needed at headquarters? For low-level personnel, a summons by the commanding officer to headquarters would cause you "to shake in your boots," as Callie put it. Nervously, she went to see the commanding officer and perhaps to get answers for why she remained in the barracks. The officer asked Callie, "Do you know why you are here?" The officer told Callie that her unit went off to Europe, and she was left off the manifest by accident.

Callie's unit left her behind, and the officer gave Callie two options that day: catch up with her unit or go back home to Philadelphia. It was a difficult decision for Callie. She wanted to be home for Christmas, like every other soldier in the military. Callie chose to return to Philadelphia, and the special orders were written up by the officer. Callie got reprieve from military service, but the break did not last long.

A WAC Serves Tuskegee

Callie spent Christmas 1945 with her family in Philadelphia. She enjoyed her holiday, but she did not stay home for long. She soon found her way to a recruiting center and signed up for duty again. After going through the entrance procedures, the military assigned Callie to Lockbourne Airforce Base in Columbus, Ohio. In Lockbourne, Callie encountered the Tuskegee Airmen for the first time. Under the command of Benjamin O. Davis Jr., Lockbourne was one of the main bases for the Tuskegee Airmen.

General Davis remains one of the most prominent African Americans to serve with the Tuskegee Airmen. With an infantry background, in May 1941, he learned to fly at Moton Field, the primary flight facility for African American pilot candidates in the US Air Corps, located in Tuskegee.

Captain Benjamin O. Davis entering an experimental trainer. *National Archives.*

He then took command of the 99th Fighter Squadron of the Tuskegee Airmen. The United States entered the war, and Davis led the men into combat above the skies of North Africa and the Italian Peninsula. As the war progressed, Davis assumed command of the 332nd Fighter Squadron, another group of Tuskegee Airmen, and served with it for the remainder of the war in Europe. Except for a brief stint with another group in the immediate postwar years, Davis returned to command the 332nd Fighter Squadron in Lockbourne.

Callie likes to dispel the popular misconception among her friends, family and colleagues that she worked directly for General Davis. The airbase assigned Callie to work within Wing Headquarters for the 332nd Fighter Group. She worked as the headquarters stenographer. A stenographer's duties consisted of executing communications for the entire base except for the commanding officer, working on special orders and partaking in court martials for men. Her entire unit fell under the jurisdiction of the Third Air Force.

The Tuskegee pilots and ground crews left a lasting impression on Callie. She remembers the men of Tuskegee just wanting to do their duty and defend their country. Everyone felt that the United States "was their country," and African Americans wanted to do their part in defending it against tyranny just as much as any other American. "My opinion now and then…these were people conducting themselves in a professional manner and doing what they knew how to do and doing what they knew they had to do," Callie declared. Her experiences as an African American in the military allowed her to relate to the Tuskegee veterans.

Callie enjoyed great respect in Lockbourne. On many occasions, Callie ate in the officer's mess hall. Her work kept her occupied well into the night and sometimes only the officer mess hall remained open. Callie held the privilege as headquarters stenographer to request a meal from the mess hall chef after closing. But she never felt comfortable disturbing the chef if officers were nice enough to ask Callie to accompany them. "My name would be mud," Callie recollects, "if I woke the chef up." Regularly, she sat and ate with the officers as equals. At the time, officers had to pay for their meals on base, and the officers took care of Callie's bill.

Callie and her friends enjoyed days off in Columbus. The enlisted folks would go into town and spend their monthly salaries. Callie and her friends once went to see a movie in the local theater. Halfway through the movie, the group realized that they needed to catch the bus back to base. If they did not catch the bus, they would be stranded and "up the creek without a paddle." They raced to catch the bus, and the movie theater politely refunded their money because they could not finish the movie. The movie theater experience illustrated the accepting atmosphere in Lockbourne, according to Callie. She enjoyed her years in the military. Callie's time in Lockbourne seemed more similar to her experiences growing up in Philadelphia than her first encounter with the segregated military.

African Americans of the Women's Army Corps (WACs). *National Archives.*

Philadelphia's Marian Anderson performing for a group of WACs and soldiers. *National Archives.*

One of her vivid experiences at Lockbourne happened when a pilot crashed during training exercises. Commanders from Third Air Force Headquarters came to investigate the crash, and Callie tagged along as Lockbourne's stenographer. She traveled with the officers to the countryside, about a few hours journey from the military base. When she arrived, Callie quickly took to her duties of stenographer, writing shorthand of the officers' interviews with the locals. Owners of the property and witnesses provided depositions on the crash. Callie used Gregg shorthand style and filled two steno pads. After the long day of testimony, Callie and the officers returned to Lockbourne.

She remembers the scene of transcribing the steno pads of the incident with the two officers from Third Airforce watching over her. The men paced back and forth while chain-smoking cigarettes. "How much longer?" the men constantly asked Callie, but she diligently and precisely worked to transcribe her steno pads from the depositions. In the wee hours of the morning, Callie finally finished transcribing the notes, and the two officers rushed out of the office. She felt exhausted but was relieved that the job was over.

After two weeks, Callie got word that headquarters wanted to see her. "What the dickens" did they want on her day off? When she arrived at headquarters, Callie encountered a surprise. Her commanding officer sat with the two "nut heads" that worked on the plane crash. The men looked despondent. Her captain told Callie that the two officers from Third Airforce lost her transcriptions and needed Callie to rewrite the depositions for them. She could not believe their incompetence and already knew the difficulty of this task.

To transcribe shorthand into typical writing, a stenographer needs to transcribe almost immediately after taking the notes, according to Callie. The plane crash happened two weeks prior, and Callie knew that she would struggle to understand notes she took that day. Conversations are fluid, with people interjecting and talking over each other, and a stenographer needs to keep up with that. Sometimes a talented stenographer will just write a dash or a squiggly line, and if transcribed right away, the stenographer will know what was meant during the job. Despite the predicted difficulty, she tackled the problem head-on.

Like the last time, the men paced back and forth, filling the air with smoke, as Callie solved their problem. She worked through her shorthand and, to the best of her ability, tried to understand what she meant. She spent a few hours on the matter, with the two officers breathing down her neck. After much meticulous reading, Callie finished the new transcriptions of the plane crash. She admits that she must have left out "very important words," but with the time between the second transcription and the interviews, Callie did everything she could. The gentlemen left satisfied, and Callie swore never to write in shorthand again. To this day, she keeps her promise.

SERVING VETERANS

Callie's experiences at Lockbourne and in the military opened opportunities after her service ended. In 1950, she left the military and moved back to Philadelphia. She went to Temple University for a period before a family issue caused her to drop out of classes. She needed to seek a full-time job and figured she had two options for employment: the Veterans Affairs office (VA) or Social Security office. During this time, veterans of the military received preferential treatment for government jobs. Callie sent her application to the VA and started working immediately.

At the VA, she worked in the insurance division and later the data processing division. She worked in administration and helped veterans with their insurance policies, billings and death cases. One of her main jobs involved using a new tool: the computer. Starting in 1951 and 1952, Callie helped establish the new infrastructure. Workers brought in the new equipment and prepared the rooms. She remembers the massive rooms dedicated to the new data processing. These data processing rooms consisted of massive mainframes atop grated floors to circulate the air conditioning in the rooms. Four rooms in the facility turned into data processing centers.

The new technology at the Veterans Affairs office required workers to be trained, and Callie joined many of her fellow workers in learning how to operate the machines. Keypunch operators put the information in by hand to synthesize the data, which turned out sheets of paper with information about specific veterans. The new technology took time to understand. The workers needed to take their time with the machines to avoid making any errors, though, eventually, the work turned into a "piece of cake," as Callie put it. The new technology became integral to the work at the VA, and the computers helped Callie with her administration work.

The computers helped process the death cases at the VA—one of Callie's main concerns in the office. When a file came into the VA about a veteran who died, Callie went to the computer to retrieve all the data about the specific veteran. The death cases involved whether an insurance payment would go to the family. In some cases, Callie and other co-workers needed to disapprove cases. The family would then go to a local congressman or the VA itself and try to overturn the rejection. Callie went over many insurance policies with "a fine-tooth comb" to try to help the families receive their money. She helped a lot of veterans' families and got "very good at" understanding the legal and bureaucratic nonsense around the insurance claims. She calls her time at the VA an "interesting and hard job."

At the same time, Callie went to work part time at Wanamaker's Department Store, today a Macy's, in downtown Philadelphia. The great bronze eagle dominated the Wanamaker's Department Store as a local landmark. The phrase "meet me at the eagle" holds a lot of meaning to Callie and other Philadelphians of the time. The Wanamaker's job gave her a chance to earn social security when she got older. Much like at the VA, Callie worked diligently in the men's clothing department. She earned the respect of her co-workers and upper management. Her time at Wanamaker's seemed to give Callie a reprieve from the stress of the VA, but that did not affect her work ethic. Callie's military training and time growing up in a Quaker neighborhood continued to influence her work ethic.

In the late 1960s, Callie became reacquainted with the Tuskegee Airmen. Years before, Callie worked in close concert with the Airmen in Columbus, Ohio, and those experiences at Lockbourne stuck with her. Philadelphia's Channel 10 put a notice in the city newspapers aimed at all African Americans who trained at Tuskegee University. The callout asked for pilots, mechanics, doctors and whoever else held associations with Tuskegee. For several weeks, the newspaper article ran.

Many in Philadelphia answered the call and soon began meeting at the television station on a regular basis. The group formed through the newspaper articles and word of mouth. More than one hundred men started meeting, and the chapter grew. Callie went to these initial meetings because of her association with the Tuskegee at Lockbourne. After meeting at the Channel 10 building, the Philadelphia chapter moved to a local hall. Like G. Naomi, Callie entered at the ground floor of the organization and remained a part of the group for decades.

The men treated Callie with great respect. Though she was not a formal member from Tuskegee, Callie experienced many of the same trials and tribulations of working within the military during the 1940s. The chapter knew Callie served at Lockbourne, and many viewed her as a Tuskegee Airman for her service with the 332nd Air Wing. She compares being included as a Tuskegee Airman with "being a member of a family."

Philadelphia chapter of Tuskegee Airmen, May 2019. *Philadelphia Chapter, Tuskegee Airmen.*

The hierarchy of the group was formed with elected officials. The Philadelphia chapter existed within a network of a national organization and it kicked up funds to help with the costs of running the national organization. The Philadelphia chapter was officially chartered in 1967, with Milton Richardson as president, Wesley Walker as vice-president and Nathanial Stewart as treasurer. Callie served as the organization's first secretary and stayed in the position for twenty-two years. She kept the times of the meetings—never in shorthand, of course—and acted as a general organizer.

She loved her job as the secretary, but the group convinced her to become president. She served as chapter president for a little less than a month before resigning to return to her secretary position. Callie felt that a woman should not be president of a "male-oriented organization." The Tuskegee veterans "did all this history making, not me," as Callie recollects. But Callie remained instrumental as secretary and left her mark on the Philadelphia chapter. The chapter still holds many of the documents—letters, attendances and archival books—that Callie created during her tenure as secretary.

As of 2019, Callie has moved away from Philadelphia, but she remains in contact with the Philadelphia chapter through her family and friends. She worked with the group until the day she finally left Philadelphia, and despite being far away, Callie still goes to Tuskegee reunions and functions. She remembers the people of the group most of all as the bedrock of the Tuskegee Chapter. Her view on the importance of Tuskegee veterans remains as strong as ever. The Tuskegee veterans destroyed the War Department's prejudicial views on African American pilots and earned their place in history, according to Callie. She is very proud of and passionate about Tuskegee veterans and her association with the group.

G. Naomi and Callie worked within the group at the same time, but their two jobs only occasionally intertwined. Whether they knew it at the time, Tuskegee would remain a part of them for the rest of their lives. Their history with the group remains an important part of the Tuskegee experience. Both women served as foundations for the Philadelphia chapter and helped the chapter in amazing ways. The important roles of two women within the predominantly male group show the inclusiveness and openness of Tuskegee University veterans. Today, the group has evolved beyond the male-oriented organization and continues to exist through the remaining veterans and family members of deceased members.

2

LEARNING TO FLY

The Trainers of Tuskegee

By Michael J. Weiss

When people think of the Tuskegee Airmen, they think of the intrepid black pilots who overcame racism and adversity to become one of the most decorated air force units of World War II. Men who fiercely fought the Axis powers of Europe to protect their country with their famous red-tailed fighter planes. Soldiers who also fought racism and sought to prove that African American men could fight just as hard as any white pilot. While the fighter pilots themselves are an essential part of the story, there were plenty of other noncombat personnel who made an impact. An important group of people often left out of the overall narrative are the African American men who trained the pilots.

HAIL TO THE "CHIEF" OF TUSKEGEE

It is impossible to tell the story of the civilian trainers without highlighting Charles Alfred "The Chief" Anderson Sr.'s contributions to black aviation. Anderson, born in 1907, spent his early life in Bryn Mawr, Pennsylvania. He was an only child and often spent time in Staunton, Virginia, with his grandmother. Anderson desired to become a pilot and would not let anything get in the way of achieving his dreams.

Anderson first attempted to attend flight school, but the color of his skin resulted in rejection. The Pets Aviation School accepted him but revoked his acceptance shortly after learning he was black. He also attempted to join the Pennsylvania National Guard, which rejected him for the same reason. Because of the prevailing racial attitudes of the time, Anderson had to figure out another way to learn how to fly.

He decided to take out a loan from the bank and used that money to purchase a Velie Monocoupe to teach himself how to fly. In addition to flying his own plane, he also accompanied Russell Thaw on his flights to Atlantic City, New Jersey. Thaw was an experienced pilot and often borrowed Anderson's plane. Anderson was so intent on learning how to fly that not even the two plane crashes he experienced could stop him.

By the end of 1929, The Chief Anderson knew enough about flying to pursue his private pilot's license. After all of his hard work, Anderson became one of the first black men in the United States to earn a private pilot's license. This marked the beginning of Anderson's incredible life as a pilot and civilian trainer.

After finally receiving his license, Anderson set about breaking down racial barriers and opening the field of aviation to other black men. Anderson continued his training with World War I veteran Ernst H. Buehl. Buehl worked as a transcontinental airmail pilot and later owned three airports. In 1932, with the help of Buehl, Anderson got his commercial flying license, which enabled him to transport passengers.

Buehl had to intercede on Anderson's behalf when the flight inspector refused to examine Anderson. During one of his many trips to Atlantic City, Anderson encountered a black surgeon named Dr. Albert Forsythe. Forsythe became Anderson's friend and financier and helped him in his purchase of another aircraft. Anderson's business would see some success, but white customers tended to stay away.

Dr. Albert E. Forsythe was born on February 25, 1897, in Nassau, Bahamas. He later moved to Port Antonio, Bahamas, where his father became a respected civil engineer. Forsythe immigrated to the United States at the age of fifteen to study architecture at the Tuskegee Institute. He continued his education at the University of Illinois and the University of Toledo.

Looking to continue his education, Forsythe enrolled at McGill University Medical School in Canada. Upon earning his medical degree, he moved to Atlantic City, where he opened a medical practice. Forsythe and Anderson would become trailblazers in black aviation. They achieved fame that would follow them throughout their lives.

Although Anderson never searched for fame, fame always found him. In 1933, Forsythe and Anderson flew from Atlantic City to Los Angeles,

California, and back. This was the first transcontinental flight completed by African American pilots in United States history. The flight took three days, and they made a total of fifty stops. The two men also encountered Charles Lindbergh on this trip.

Looking back on their flight together, Forsythe stated that "it was something that had to be done to break down all the restrictions." Anderson and Forsythe would also fly goodwill flights to the Bahamas, Cuba, Jamaica, Haiti, the Dominican Republic, Puerto Rico, the Virgin Islands, Granada and Trinidad. The Black Press enthusiastically followed Anderson's exploits and celebrated his accomplishments. While Forsythe ultimately returned to his medical practice, Anderson continued to fly.

After marrying his wife, Gertrude Nelson, Anderson took a job as a flight instructor at Howard University's CPTP. He worked there until the Tuskegee Institute invited him to become its chief flight instructor at Kennedy Field. There, Anderson earned the nickname of "Chief." He trained many people, including his old neighborhood acquaintance Roscoe Draper. During a trip to Alabama to meet with a black philanthropic organization, First Lady Eleanor Roosevelt visited Kennedy Field.

The training of black fighter pilots for the Ninety-Ninth Fighter Squadron was slated to begin in April 1941. Roosevelt personally asked Chief Anderson to take her on a flight. He graciously agreed. The ride was a great success and the first lady praised Anderson and the other black pilots for their skills. This event was highly publicized, and it enabled Anderson to prove on a national scale that black men were just as capable as others of flying planes.

The first class of black pilots that Anderson taught at the Tuskegee Institute became the instructors that taught the rest of the Tuskegee Airmen. A few miles north of Kennedy Field, the U.S. Army Air Corps helped the school build a larger airfield named Mooton Field. Mooton Field would be the first military installation built by a black construction company. Anderson's students kept in close contact with him and often sent him letters from the front.

After the war, Anderson remained at Mooton Field and continued to teach black pilots how to fly. He mostly taught Reserve Officers' Training Corps (ROTC) cadets and private students. In 1967, Anderson helped found the Negro Airmen International (NAI) and received many awards for his numerous achievements. The NAI is currently the oldest African American piloting organization, and it operated a summer flight academy for black students until 1989. In 1991, Anderson was inducted in the Alabama Aviation Hall of Fame, nearly a half century after his World War II service.

Tuskegee Airmen Museum, Tuskegee, Alabama. *The George F. Landegger Collection of Alabama Photographs in Carol M. Highsmith's America, Library of Congress, Prints and Photographs Division.*

The Chief's career is spectacular for any pilot. It is even more impressive when one considers the obstacles he overcame—for himself and others. The Chief paved the way for all future black pilots, and his contribution to the Tuskegee Airmen cannot be overstated. His influence proved considerable on Roscoe Draper, who strove to emulate him while serving as a civilian trainer. Anderson passed away from natural causes at the age of eighty-nine in 1996.

THE "COACH" OF TUSKEGEE

Civilian trainers taught the Tuskegee Airmen in the first phase of training. The trainers were black men who each had earned a private pilot's license. They served as the earliest examples of African American men learning to fly planes. One of these trainers was Roscoe "Coach" Draper of Haverford, Pennsylvania. He was one of many Tuskegee Airmen from the Greater Philadelphia area. While Draper never became a fighter pilot, his efforts proved instrumental in molding the Tuskegee Airmen.

Draper was born on May 14, 1919, on the Pennsylvania Main Line. He grew up with six siblings on a farm that used to sit on Buck Lane in

Mr. Roscoe Draper, the "Coach." *Philadelphia Chapter, Tuskegee Airmen.*

Haverford, Pennsylvania. The Drapers moved around frequently and lived in Bryn Mawr and Radnor Township, Pennsylvania, and Maryland, before their eventual return to Haverford. Draper's parents were both domestics who were responsible for housework and maintenance. After giving birth to her seventh child, Draper's mother passed away. Roscoe was only nine years old. The Draper family permanently returned to Haverford when Roscoe entered the seventh grade. Draper's aunt, his father's sister, raised Roscoe and his siblings following their mother's death.

From an early age, Draper was hardworking and tenacious. He was an excellent student and graduated from Haverford High School with honors.

Living in Haverford, he claims that he never experienced "anything out of the ordinary" when it came to racism and segregation. Although Draper had not encountered significant racism, African Americans across the United States were either legally or de facto segregated. They also remained barred from many professions. Following high school, Roscoe Draper did not have an outright desire to fly planes and was not even sure that he could afford college. He finally considered pursuing a degree when a friend told him he could work while attending college.

Draper chose to enroll at the Hampton Institute in Hampton, Virginia, as an auto mechanic. The Hampton Institute was a black college that was founded by black and white men from the American Missionary Association shortly after the Civil War to educate recently freed slaves. Draper found that he lacked the desire to become a mechanic and decided to pursue a career as a sheet metal worker. In 1939, during Draper's second year of college, the Hampton Institute opened a Civilian Pilot Training Program (CPTP). Despite harboring reservations about learning to fly, Roscoe decided to enroll in the program. It was this decision that set Roscoe Draper on the path to greatness.

The United States government established the CPTP in 1938 as a means to train university students as civilian pilots. The government hoped to increase the number of pilots at their disposal in preparation for the country's potential entry into World War II. The Civil Aeronautics Authority (CAA) chose six historically black colleges to receive funding for a civilian pilot program. The CAA selected Howard University, the Hampton Institute, Delaware State College, North Carolina A&T State University, West Virginia State College and, most notably, the Tuskegee Institute.

After a lot of hard work, Draper finally earned his private pilot's license in 1940. Out of the many students trained at the Hampton Institute, Draper was one of two men selected for the secondary course at the Tuskegee Institute. It was at Tuskegee that Draper managed to make his mark on history.

Although the CPTP had produced a lot of black civilian pilots, they remained barred by civilian airlines and were prohibited from joining the United States Army Air Corps. In 1941, the long-awaited entry into World War II occurred, following the bombing of Pearl Harbor. Like many Americans, Roscoe Draper felt compelled to join the armed forces in hopes of protecting the country he loved. He was ready and wanted to fly, so he enlisted in the U.S. Army Air Corps. His strong sense of patriotism was not enough to overcome the prejudice present in the armed forces though. The army air corps denied his application. Instead of dwelling on this, he

Chaplain Major D.L.T. Robinson with two unidentified Tuskegee flight instructors. *The Black Archives of Mid-America.*

focused on moving forward with a different plan. He decided that if he could not fly for the United States, he would train pilots who could.

Thanks to the efforts of the Tuskegee Institute, specifically George Leeward Washington, Roscoe got his chance to leave his mark on history. George L. Washington was born in Norfolk, Virginia, to a Baptist minister. He went on to get a bachelor's and master's degree in mechanical engineering from the Massachusetts Institute of Technology. Under Washington's leadership, the Tuskegee Institute grew to be one of the only schools to have a self-funded program that taught a "secondary course."

The Tuskegee Institute purchased and improved an airstrip, bought additional airplanes and hired more instructors. Before a program to train fighter pilots could be established though, black men had to be able to participate in the army air corps. This fight was spearheaded by the NAACP, which initiated a lawsuit against the U.S. Army Air Corps.

Black men had been excluded from the U.S. Army Air Corps because the military believed that they lacked the natural ability to be pilots. Army

Philadelphia Tuskegee Airmen Henry Baldwin, Aaron Watkins and Roscoe Draper.
Philadelphia Chapter, Tuskegee Airmen.

officials pointed to the complicated technical abilities required to fly planes and the overall prestige of the organization as a means of excluding black men. The NAACP and the Black Press refused to let this stand and made it into a national issue. The success of the CPTP programs provided an example of how successful African American men could be as pilots.

Draper felt "grateful to the country for giving us the opportunity to fly. I was taught at the government's expense, or else I wouldn't have made it as I was. I owe a debt of gratitude." Although their skills impressed policy makers and eventually First Lady Eleanor Roosevelt, a proponent of civil rights, the U.S. Army Air Corps still had to be forced to allow black men into their ranks.

The NAACP pointed to men like Draper who had done extremely well in the program and had been selected for the secondary course. Draper recalls his instructor saying, "These guys can really fly." Draper and the other men of the secondary course played a key role in proving that these programs could produce skilled black pilots. After exerting enough political pressure, the government of President Franklin Delano Roosevelt passed the Selective

Service Act of 1940. This act prevented the United States military from discriminating against enlisted men based on race.

Despite the opportunity, Roscoe decided not to enlist in the U.S. Army Air Force. His decision resulted from his sense that "it seemed they were done with me, and I was done with them."

Still, Roscoe Draper finally had the opportunity to put his piloting skills to use. During his time in the secondary course, Roscoe learned to fly from someone he came to respect and look up to. The man who instructed Draper was Chief Anderson. The Chief instructed the first group at the Tuskegee Institute, and Roscoe Draper was in that first African American class taught to fly at Tuskegee. Not only did Draper's dream of learning to fly come true, but he was also proud to have been taught by a black man.

Anderson was one of the first African American men to earn a private piloting license and is known today as the father of black aviation. Draper and Anderson grew up in the same town and knew one another when they were younger. Anderson's mother had been a steward at the church Draper's family attended in Bryn Mawr. When Draper speaks about Chief Anderson, his voice soars. When asked if he looked up to Anderson, Draper replied, "Yes! He was incredible."

According to Draper, "He went to unbelievable ends to prove to the world that they were wrong in their assumption that black people couldn't fly." Because Chief Anderson broke down these barriers, Draper stated, "I will always feel I owe him an awful lot, the way he opened doors for me. Chief Anderson opened doors we never could have approached otherwise." Anderson's exploits made him a household name in black homes at the time.

TUSKEGEE TRAINING

In 1942, Draper graduated from the secondary course of the Tuskegee Institute and briefly returned to the Hampton Institute to work as a flight instructor. This did not last long though, as Draper became one of ten black men selected to become an instructor for the Tuskegee Experiment, referring to the experimental nature of the program that sought to train black pilots. The military did not entirely believe that black men could fly effectively and that they simply lacked the ability. Although there were many people who wanted nothing more than for the "experiment" to fail, this never changed Draper's resolve.

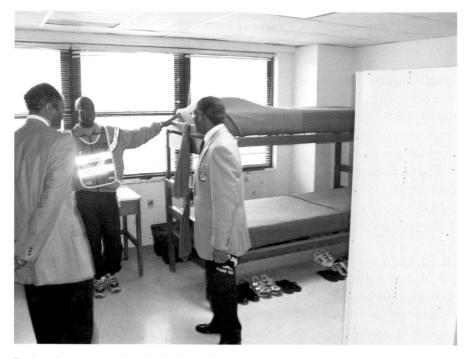

Back to the barracks. *Philadelphia Chapter, Tuskegee Airmen.*

Alongside nine other trainers, including his former mentor Chief Anderson, Draper had the job of training one thousand African American men to become fighter pilots. Like every other job Draper had been tasked with throughout his life, he faced it head-on and got the job done. Draper was responsible for teaching the initial phase of aviation training because he was a civilian pilot. He quickly earned the respect and admiration of his students and acquired his nickname, "Coach." Draper still firmly believes that the most important rule of coaching is to earn the respect of one's students.

To become a Tuskegee Airman, students had to pass four phases of training. Primary flight training was evenly split between time in the classroom and time flying. Subjects that instructors taught in the classroom phaser included the theory of flight, physics, navigation, radio procedures and aircraft recognition. When the cadets were on the airstrip, they were taught how to use checklists; how to parachute and bail-out; and how to do stalls, spins and acrobatic maneuvers. Most importantly, they were required to complete a total of 175 landings. Once cadets completed this phase of their training, they moved on to advanced training.

The final three phases of a cadet's training introduced each novice pilot to flying a military aircraft. The secondary phase provided the initial introduction to military flight. With seventy to seventy-five flight hours, pilots learned military flight techniques, how to fly in formations and how to fly cross-country and overnight. This phase lasted a total of nine weeks. The following two phases finally transitioned cadets from single engine planes to fighter planes. Trainers with a military background proved essential in the advanced phases of training. Transitioning to a military plane was no easy task.

The final lessons of the training educated pilots on the advanced maneuvers that could save their lives during combat. These advanced maneuvers included aerobatics, turns and emergency procedures. Draper trained the Tuskegee Airmen from 1942 until the war ended in 1945. His students built on the legacy of Chief Anderson and proved to the country once and for all that black men could fly just as well as white men. The in-depth training the Tuskegee Airmen received made them some of the most well-trained American pilots during the war. Although Draper only participated in the primary phase of the pilot training, his instruction allowed the cadets to learn the basics of flight.

THE "COACH'S" GUYS

Draper "coached" many famous Tuskegee airmen during his time as a civilian trainer. His most famous student would be Lee Archer. He always felt that Archer had incredible talent and was not surprised when he was awarded the title of Ace. Archer would be the only Tuskegee Airmen to achieve this honor and flew an impressive total of 169 missions. Roscoe, true to form, remained humble when speaking about Archer's success: "He was a great pilot…he trained with me, but I had nothing to do with that." For his bravery Archer would be awarded the Distinguished Flying Cross, along with many other commendations, by the United States Armed Forces.

Archer grew up in Yonkers, New York, and later moved to Harlem in New York City. Upon graduating from New York University in 1941, he enlisted in the U.S. Army Air Corps. Archer became a Tuskegee Airman in December 1942. He served in Italy during the war and was responsible for strafing ground targets and escorting bombers. Archer's most successful mission occurred on October 12, 1944. Archer and six other men of the 332nd Fighter Group flew from Budapest, Hungary, to Bratislava, Slovakia,

A break well deserved. *Library of Congress.*

on a strafing mission. Archer flew in a plane named the *Macon Bell* and shot down a total of three German Me-109s. The 332nd received credit for shooting down a total of nine enemy aircrafts that day.

Following the end of the war, Archer remained in the Air Force until 1970 and assumed countless roles. He trained air force reserve pilots at New York University, held numerous leadership positions and served in the French Liaison Office and Supreme Headquarters Allied Powers Europe and was a chief or executive in three international military organizations.

After his impressive career in the armed forces concluded, Archer went on to a successful civilian life. He served as vice-president for urban affairs at

General Foods Corporation, CEO of North Street Capital Corporation and chairman of the Hudson Commercial Corporation. He also helped establish Essence Communications Incorporated and *Black Enterprise* magazine. Archer passed away on January 27, 2010, at the age of ninety.

Another student of Draper's was Charles McGee. Like Archer, McGee served in Italy and belonged to the 332nd Fighter Group. He routinely flew over Austria, Germany and the Balkans on escort and strafing missions. On August 23, 1944, McGee encountered the German Luftwaffe on an escort mission over Czechoslovakia. He engaged the formation and shot down a German Fw 190.

Following the end of World War II, McGee became a career officer in the United States Air Force and flew during the Korean and Vietnam Wars. He has flown a total of 409 combat missions, 139 of them occurring during World War II. Of Draper's students, 450 fought overseas in the 99th Pursuit Squadron and the 332nd Fighter Group. Draper was impressed by the skill they had acquired when they returned from the war and exclaimed, "Guys we taught came back from the war and had more experience than we had."

Postwar Life

During his training of the Tuskegee Airmen, Draper met the love of his life. According to Draper, at that time, he was in his twenties and "was flying airplanes and meeting pretty girls." He met the future Mary Malone Draper in Tuskegee when she was working as a secretary to the head of the agricultural program at Tuskegee University. She had previously worked as a secretary to the Hampton Institute's dean of women. He believed that they were "a match made in the heavens." He married her in 1944, and they remained happily wed until her death.

Ever the trainer, Draper attempted to teach his wife how to fly. Mary did not take well to flying and happily left Tuskegee after the war concluded and Roscoe was no longer needed. He went on to have two children with Mary. Roscoe misses his co-pilot dearly and stated, "It's been a different, unpleasant role making it without her."

In 1945, World War II ended, and the United States and its allies emerged victorious from one of the most destructive conflicts in world history. Draper believes that America, and more specifically the administrations of Franklin Delano Roosevelt and Harry Truman, "did the best they could given the circumstances they were given."

The Tuskegee group received 150 commendations from countries all around the world. More importantly, they were a sterling example that black people could rise above the racism and segregation that existed in the United States if they worked hard enough. The Tuskegee Airmen also paved the way for the desegregation of the military.

Despite all their achievements and their military service, the Tuskegee Airmen returned to a segregated country that still viewed them as second-class citizens. The Double V Campaign, victory over racism both at home and abroad, was not won when the war ended. Victory over segregation was not achieved. Although critics who had directly encountered the Tuskegee Airmen had been silenced, there remained many people throughout the country who would never accept their accomplishments.

African Americans throughout the southern United States were still forced to live entirely separate from their white counterparts due to Jim Crow laws. In the North, including in Philadelphia, de facto segregation persisted. Black pilots returned home to find that there were few civilian aviation jobs available to them. Many companies unfortunately preferred white pilots over their black counterparts.

Roscoe Draper officially left his job as a civilian trainer in 1946. He returned to his hometown of Haverford, Pennsylvania, and in 1947, he became an employee of the U.S. Postal Service in Philadelphia. Roscoe Draper did not receive a hero's welcome and simply folded back into life as an average working man. This was to his liking though—he never wanted the fame or the accolades he would earn later in life. He enjoyed working as a night supervisor and earned a good living. He "loved the post office because it provided for us." To supplement his income, he also worked part time at a liquor store.

Despite working a job that did not require him to fly planes, he always renewed his currency and ratings. For the next twenty years he only flew as a part-time instructor between his shifts at the post office. He would fly out of the Old Star Airport in Langhorne, Pennsylvania, before it became the Oxford Valley Mall. One of his students was a local woman named Elaine Huf, who began lessons with him at the age of nineteen in 1967. Similar to the students of his past, he quickly earned her respect and admiration. By 1968, she had earned her private pilot's license and would go on to earn a few other aviation licenses. Roscoe, always the humble man, never spoke of how he had trained the Tuskegee Airmen. According to Huf, "He never spoke of his accomplishments. To me, he was just Roscoe, my beloved flight instructor."

All ears. Getting briefed. *Library of Congress.*

Draper left the postal service in 1970 to start a career at the Federal Aviation Administration (FAA). At the FAA, he worked as a pilot examiner and an accident investigator until his retirement. On top of teaching flight lessons, Draper continued to expand his own knowledge of flying. At the age of sixty he earned his helicopter rating. Draper loved the helicopter because "when you're hovering, you have to do almost nothing—and I can do almost nothing better than anyone I know." Even at his current age, Roscoe maintains the currency of his ratings and licenses. He stated that flying was "great to begin with, and then they were paying me for it, too."

In 2019, Mr. Draper turned one hundred years old and remained in good spirits. He rides an exercise bike five or six times a week and only eats enough to stay healthy. Draper still drives a car and flies planes as a secondary pilot. He was one of the first individuals to train African American pilots who would serve their country in World War II and is one of the oldest living Tuskegee Airmen.

Draper remains in great physical health and still proudly sports a light blue blazer that commemorates the Tuskegee Airmen. He has received many honors for his service to his country, but he remains extremely humble about his time as a trainer. The Philadelphia chapter of the Black Pilots of America took his legacy as their namesake. Draper chose not to attend a medal ceremony in 2007 because he felt that the men who had fought in the war deserved it more.

During his time coaching the young black pilots, Draper never imagined he would become part of an important chapter of World War II. In his own words, "It never crossed my mind that we'd be considered pioneers." Draper never failed to earn the respect of his students and enjoyed his time teaching the Tuskegee Airmen. He doesn't view himself as a hero though and instead says that he was just a man who wanted to fly planes. Ironically, the humility that prevents Roscoe Draper from viewing himself as a hero is the same trait that truly makes him one.

The Tuskegee Airmen were first and foremost men who simply wanted to achieve their dreams and do what they loved. In their pursuit of happiness, they ended up influencing the desegregation of the armed forces and breaking down plenty of racial barriers. The civilian trainers were especially instrumental in paving the way for the future success of black aviation.

3

THE BOMBERS

Bringing the Fight Home

By Michael Kowalski

BECOMING BOMBERS

Bert Levy was on his way to work at the stables along Philadelphia's Belmont Avenue. It was a misty December day, around ten o'clock in the morning, and he had received a call from Fannie the night before asking him to come by the next morning to trail-break a few horses. They had just received a shipment of new ponies, and she wanted Bert to get the horses familiar with the trail so that their clients wouldn't have to worry about where they were going and could focus solely on staying atop their horses. Bert was an instructor at Fannie's stable and taught kids from the Main Line how to ride horses after school. As a bonus for working as an instructor Bert got to ride the horses whenever he wanted so long as he took care of any students who showed up. He figured he would head over to Fannie's stable early that morning, work with the horses and take a ride himself, then head home and settle in for a lazy Sunday.

After riding up and down the trail a few times, Bert and his friend Jimmy, who also worked at the stable, stripped the gear off the horses, brushed them down and began their walk home. They made their way toward the Fortieth Street trolley, hoping to pick it up and expedite their journey. Bert lived about five miles from the stable on South Fifteenth Street, and while he could walk the distance, the brisk air suggested otherwise. As they walked south on Belmont Avenue Bert and Jimmy saw an elegantly dressed woman wearing black from head to toe in what they thought must be her best church

Sky over Tuskegee. *Philadelphia Chapter, Tuskegee Airmen.*

attire. She saw them and began to cross the street and make her way toward the two men. As she waved to them, both Bert and Jimmy checked behind them to see to whom she might be waving, soon realizing it was the attention of each that she meant to attract. As she crossed the street, she yelled, "I sure [hope] you boys don't have to go!" Bert and Jimmy shared a glance and silently agreed she must have had too much sacramental wine at church because they were sure they had no idea what she was talking about. They walked on, picked up the trolley and headed home.

Bert and Jimmy got lost in conversation while riding the trolley and missed their stop. Realizing their mistake, they got off at the Broad Street stop and began their walk back. Both men felt the winter chill and decided they could use a cup of coffee. Bert and Jimmy spotted a White Castle restaurant in their path and chose to stop in. As they approached, they could see steam fogging up the windows and a multitude of customers hunched around the radio. They could hear that the president was making an address. Something had happened at Pearl Harbor. Bert was sure that he had never heard of the place, but once he found out about what happened there that morning, he was determined to do his part. The very next morning he headed to the recruitment office.

James Robert Williams spent many of his younger years on a farm in Virginia. He was an only child, and his mother passed away when he was three years old. But that is not to say he lacked a family; James was raised with his aunts and uncles, all living under his grandparent's roof, with his aunt acting as a surrogate mother. He could recall all of them living together—all of his cousins feeling more like brothers and sisters.

One day the house caught fire and burned down. His grandfather, a local blacksmith, moved the family to Pennsylvania where James's father worked at the Coatesville Steel Mill. James, his aunts, uncles and cousins all moved to Warner Avenue in Bryn Mawr, a predominantly black neighborhood at the time. Many neighbors worked for wealthy families on the Main Line as domestics, gardeners and butlers, but all were unified by one thing: Reverend Younger of the Saints Memorial Baptist Church. James and his neighbors would go to church every Sunday and listen to sermons on becoming exceptional men, striving for their goals and working harder and longer than everyone else. In a world that judged by color rather than character, these sermons resonated as sound advice. It was a message that many in the neighborhood took to heart; several of James's childhood friends would become successful—one became a professional football player, another a three-star general. Others became doctors, lawyers and servicemen and women. It was a close-knit group for several years. On Prospect Avenue they would dodge cars and gather to play baseball, football and hockey. When the weather got in their way, they'd play marbles.

The group's members could see the front door of Memorial Baptist Church where they played, and many of James's childhood memories revolved around that church and the community it fostered. James became close friends with a neighbor (and future three-star general) Julius Becton during his early years in the neighborhood. Becton's mother called him "her third son." He'd eventually be the best man at Becton's wedding.

James began attending Lower Merion High School in 1939, and he excelled in academics and athletics. He became an All-State tackle for the football team and ran sprints and hurdles for indoor track and field, where he made it to state competition. During the summers, he worked as a dogcatcher and milkman to earn some spending money. Despite his athletic prowess, James was always truly an academic. From a young age, he knew he wanted to become a doctor. His career in medicine would have to wait, however, as it was during his high school years that James found his other dream: flying.

Halfway through James's junior year, Pearl Harbor changed the American landscape. Thousands of Americans enlisted in all branches of the military in response. As the United States entered World War II, the military made an effort to increase its ranks even further. Shortly after the surprise attack, General Henry Arnold made an appearance at Lower Merion High School, convincing dozens of James's classmates to enlist in the military. James had always had a passion for flying, and through black newspapers like the *Chicago Defender*, *Pittsburgh Courier* and *Baltimore Afro American*, he had heard of the Tuskegee Airmen. It was their ranks that James wanted to join. But James wasn't the only one with ambitions of becoming a "Fly Boy."

On December 8, Bert Levy made his way to Thirteenth and Market Street in Philadelphia. He passed Wannamaker's Department Store and walked toward the Sun Ray Drug Store. He made his way up the stairs to his destination, an army recruitment office. Once he entered, he told the recruiter that he wanted to join the army. The recruiter asked him if he knew how to cook. Bert responded, "No, I want to get into a unit that does the flying," to which the recruiter replied, "We don't have any colored people in that yet."

Bert had always been passionate about aviation and always loved the sound of a plane flying overhead. He didn't want to join the army just for the sake of doing so—he wanted to follow his passion and become a pilot. Despite the demand for new recruits, the army did not allow African Americans to enlist in specific fields. It more readily assigned them to whatever openings they needed. Bert knew he didn't need to enlist that day, so he told the recruiter to forget it. There were other recruitment offices in the city. Bert was determined to find one that would let him follow his passion.

After trying at a few more recruitment offices and meeting with the same answer, Bert went to the *Philadelphia Tribune*, the oldest continuously

Honoring Philadelphia Tuskegee bomber pilot Reverend Henry Baldwin. *Philadelphia Chapter, Tuskegee Airmen.*

Past and present. *Philadelphia Chapter, Tuskegee Airmen.*

published black newspaper in the country, to notify them of what was going on. His story, far from unique, along with mounting pressure from other sectors of the black community, began to catch the ear of people in influential positions. Bert eventually found his way to the recruitment office on Third and Chestnut in Old City Philadelphia. While waiting in line, he overheard some of the men talking about an examination for people who wanted to join the army air corps that would be administered soon.

Mounting pressure from all sides of the black community brought change. The government began to administer an air corps enlistment test that would allow people to join regardless of race as long as their scores were sufficient. Bert took the exam in July 1942. It had taken him six months, but Bert finally had his chance to enter the army on his terms. As the test proctors read the names of those who'd taken the exam, those who passed were sent to the armory on Thirty-Second and Lancaster Avenue in West Philadelphia for further examination. Those who failed were sent home.

Bert anxiously waited to hear his named called. When they finally announced his name, Bert was ecstatic to hear them direct him to the armory. He knew that he would pass any test they gave him from here on out. After passing his physical, he was admitted to the army air corps. His dream of being a pilot would be realized. His twenty-six-year career in the army had begun.

Much like Bert Levy, James Williams's attempts to join the army would not be met with initial success. His first attempt at joining the air corps ostensibly failed because of his weight, but James knew that the few pounds he had to lose wouldn't have mattered had he been white. When the recruiter told him that he was over the acceptable limit, James told him that he'd be back in two weeks, under the weight limit. The recruiter replied "OK, come on back, boy." Following his rejection, James heard of the entrance exam that would allow him to become a member of the air corps, and, like Bert Levy, following the exam, his name was called, and he was sent to the armory. There he passed the physical (with a few pounds to spare) and was on his way to the army air corps.

IN THE ARMY NOW

Both Bert Levy and James Williams would make their way into the 477th Bombardment Group. It would be the first bomber unit in the air corps

Reverend Henry Baldwin, the spirit of Tuskegee in Philadelphia. *Philadelphia Chapter, Tuskegee Airmen.*

to be staffed with African American pilots and crews. After persistent pressure from the Black Press, the NAACP, voters and even his wife, Eleanor, Franklin Roosevelt authorized African American military aviation programs. Shortly thereafter, the flying school at Tuskegee University was created. While Tuskegee pilots succeeded in the field, fighting enemies abroad and skeptics at home, the army was reluctant to begin a bomber program. It cited the greater technical difficulty with bomber training and clung to the perception that black pilots would not be able to handle the high level of complexity.

General Henry "Hap" Arnold, who convinced James Williams and many of his high school classmates to join the war effort, failed as an advocate for James and other young men of color. He used his position as head of the army air forces to try to end the initiative to allow blacks to serve as bombers before it could get started. But mounting political pressure proved too much for him. It would take years, however, for the 477th to have the opportunity to conduct full combat training missions. The unit was activated on January 15, 1944.

By the winter of 1944, the 477th was stationed at Selfridge Field near Detroit and began to conduct combat training. Winter weather greatly limited their

General Henry "Hap" Arnold. *National Archives.*

ability to do so. Unfortunately, weather was not the only enemy the bombers confronted. Their commander, Colonel Robert Selway, laid down as many roadblocks as he could. Promotions readily went to white officers and staff, while black promotions proved quite rare. Selfridge Field had a history of racial tension, as evidenced by an incident at the officers' club on January 1, 1944. Defying army regulations that stated all officers at the post had a right to full membership, Colonel William L. Boyd turned away several black officers who attempted entry. Though against military regulations, this type of segregation was far from rare and received endorsement from high-ranking base commanders.

Race riots that took place in neighboring Detroit, along with growing conflict over access to the officers' club, led the air corps to move the 477th to Godman Field, Kentucky. This new location promised greater training opportunities, but it did little to end the racial tensions. The bombers trained with B-25s in preparation for combat missions. Both Bert Levy and James Williams became certified bomber pilots, but neither saw combat in World

War II. The B-25 became one of the most reliable tools in the army air corps's arsenal, seeing action in both the European and Pacific theaters. Different variations of the plane could even be outfitted with a 75 mm cannon for antiship missions. Despite its expertise with one of the army's most efficient weapons, the 477th never entered either theater.

One of the perks of moving to the new airfield was that the officers would have full use of the officers' club on base. This luxury was denied to them in the past. But racial tensions far from subsided. While black officers could access the club on Godman, white supervisors used the segregated facilities at Fort Knox. Since the black officers were not assigned to Fort Knox, they were not allowed access and the de facto segregation of black and white officers continued. Other issues arose for the bombers in training. The move that had appeared so promising in the beginning turned sour. Godman lacked sufficient hangar space or an air-to-ground gunnery range. Again, the trainees did not receive effective training. This spurred another move, this time to Freeman Field, Indiana, in March 1945. There they found adequate grounds for their training but also the most direct racial conflict they would face.

THE FIGHT AT HOME

Hundreds of Airmen received their wings at Freeman Field, but the only conflict any of them saw during the war was at the base. While the 477th Bombardment Group had contended with discrimination from both their bases and the surrounding communities, the residents of Seymour, Indiana, proved to be more inviting, or at least tolerant. The 477th still clashed with their supervisors over the same issue they had faced at Selfridge Field— segregation in the officers' club. To keep white and black officers from using the same officers' club, Colonel Robert Selway designated one of the clubs on base for "supervisory personnel" and the other for "trainees." Selway also informed the men that the swimming pool and tennis court were off limits.

Racial tensions came to a head on April 5, 1945, as dozens of black officers decided to stand against this de facto segregation. Thirty-six black officers entered the officers' club despite an order from the assistant provost marshal that they leave. All thirty-six men were arrested by the provost marshal. The next day another twenty-one officers entered the club in protest. They, too, were arrested.

The commanders at Freeman Field attempted to save face, claiming that it was a long-standing policy for supervisors and trainees to occupy different clubs so they may set aside their rank and relax. This explanation did nothing to stop the chorus of disapproval that followed. Air force legal officers soon arrived to investigate the situation and found Colonel Selway's orders to be unclear in purpose and function. As a result, the arrested men were immediately released. That is, all but three—those who had allegedly pushed the provost marshal while entering the club. The battle against segregation began in earnest.

Following the incident, Colonel Selway issued an order for all black officers on base to sign that expressly stated which facilities they were and were not allowed to use. Signing this served as an acknowledgement that they understood the order. Many of the officers refused to sign, and in response, Colonel Selway struck the "understood" section of the order, so signing merely indicated that it had been read. Of the 422 black officers stationed at the base, 101 still refused to sign the order and later became known as the 101 Club. Each of these men were summarily flown back to Godman Field and placed under arrest. There they awaited court-martial hearings.

Refusal to sign was no small matter, and the officers knew it. Many later reported that Colonel Selway threatened them with Article 64 upon their refusal. This states that men who fail to obey a superior officer's direct order could receive the death penalty. Despite these threats, the officers stood their ground. But the officers were not alone in their fight against their superior officers, as a multitude of groups stood in their defense. Black newspapers published their story and brought light to the outrage. The NAACP and several elected officials, including Congressman Adam Clayton Powell, Congressman Louis Ludlow, Congresswoman Helen Gahagan and Senator Arthur H. Vandenberg, used their connections to push for the release of the imprisoned officers.

The pressure from both community members and government officials proved successful. In mid-April the charges against the black officers who refused to sign the order were dropped. It was not a complete victory, though, as the charges against the three officers who were accused of pushing the provost marshal remained.

Two of the officers, Lieutenants Shirley Clinton and Marsden Thompson, faced trial together. According to witnesses, the accused officers never actually touched the provost marshal, and the prosecution could not provide any solid evidence that the marshal ever actually ordered the officers not to enter. As a result, both were acquitted of all charges. The next day,

U.S. representative Adam Clayton Powell Jr. (Democrat, New York). *Library of Congress.*

Lieutenant Roger Terry faced trial, but the outcome did not go in his favor. The court acquitted him of disobeying a superior officer's lawful order but convicted him of jostling the provost marshal. He was sentenced to a fine of $150, a loss of rank and a dishonorable discharge.

By the time the trials took place, Colonel Selway had been relieved of command of the 477th and had been replaced by Lieutenant Colonel Benjamin Davis. Davis was the fourth African American to graduate from West Point and was a tried and true commander. He later became the first African American general officer in the United States Air Force. Under Davis, the entire chain of command was replaced by black officers and the 477th was moved back to Godman Field.

The 477th never saw action in the Atlantic or Pacific theaters. Its members never got to prove themselves in combat. Though many of the men had received their wings and were combat ready, the Japanese surrendered before they could be deployed. Many of the men joked that the Japanese heard they were coming and decided it was hopeless. Indeed, their greatest battle proved to be not with their enemies but with their comrades and commanders. The Freeman Field Mutiny, as it came to be called, caught the attention of not only the black community but also the military's leadership. Leaders were forced to rethink segregationist policies.

The events at Freeman Field provide a definitive example of what was known among black servicemen as the Double V campaign—victory over the racism of the enemy abroad and victory over racism at home. Over time, the men of the 101 Club, as well as the three officers taken to court, proved warranted in their actions. In 1995, the air force removed the letters of reprimand from the permanent files of the officers charged at Freeman Field, and Lieutenant Terry was granted a full pardon for his court martial, as well as the reinstatement of his rank and the return of his fine money. Ultimately, the 477th would not go down in history for its combat record against the country's enemies in World War II, but instead would make its mark in the fight against segregation in the army and air force. Though the war ended before the 477th could drop any bombs on the enemy, it still left a mark.

Bert Levy received his bomber training among the 477th at Godman Field, but not all of the airmen who received their bomber training would be located in Selfridge, Freeman or Godman Fields. James Williams trained as a single engine pilot and twin-engine bomber pilot at Tuskegee's Moton Field and received his navigator certification in Hondo, Texas, and his bombadier certification in Midland, Texas. Attaining all three certifications was rare and difficult, with only a handful of Airmen accomplishing the task. But the

Dr. James Williams, Airman and physician. *Philadelphia Chapter, Tuskegee Airmen.*

endless training cycle that Williams undertook made it possible. The bombing techniques, much like the B-25s they were training with, were innovative. This required the new pilots to learn a great deal as they went. Williams and Levy, like many others, never saw combat in the field despite this extensive training.

Flight school was very difficult for James Williams. The training was intensive and required him to learn a wide variety of skills and techniques, often in highly stressful situations. Williams's first solo flight came after he had completed a series of touch-and-go drills, which involved him taking off and immediately landing over and over again. After a few hours of this sort of training, his instructor jumped out of the plane and said to Williams, "OK, now go up there and kill yourself." Thankfully, Williams failed to do so. In a later training mission, Williams was tasked to fly low over some corn fields to simulate a bombing raid at minimal altitude. He later recalled that he flew so low that he hit corn stalks.

Despite the anxiety of his training, Williams became a skilled pilot and was assigned to fly important personnel here or there. He once flew a colonel from Tuskegee to a meeting in Washington, D.C., but during the flight, the colonel took over the controls and flew their plane right past the Washington Monument. Williams was terrified about flying so close to the monument, but the colonel was an accomplished pilot himself, and he dared not question the decision. Williams was not allowed to stay in any of the hotels in Washington, D.C., due to his race. He had to fly back to Tuskegee the very same night.

James Williams faced a number of instances much like the one in Washington, D.C., where he would be restricted by his race. On one occasion, a trip between bases, Williams along with a group of black bombers and white pilots were to take a bus to their next training facility. Upon arrival, the white pilots climbed aboard, followed by the black bombers. When the bombers attempted to set foot on the bus, the driver responded that he would not be accepting any black passengers. The pilots, in a show of camaraderie, stepped off the bus and informed the driver that he would be driving all of them or none of them. The driver relented. On another trip, Williams recalled observing German prisoners of war entering a facility from which he and his fellow bombers had just been turned away.

Bert Levy also had his share of tension while training, but what stood out to him was the level of expertise he needed to become a bomber. An understanding of physics, thrust, weight, torque, wind speed and a variety of other factors played a part in flying those planes. Pilots had to keep a close eye on their controls, and with the weight of the engine concentrated in the front of the plane, it was important for them to keep the noses up and maintain speed. The bombers had to train as pilots first to gain an understanding of aeronautics and then work their way up to twin-engine bombers like the B-25.

STANDING TALL

Levy stayed in the service until 1968. His time as a Tuskegee Airman opened doors later in his military career. With the challenges he faced came attention and recognition. He later stated, "I got a lot of breaks, and I'd go where the breaks were." Though his opportunities to fly planes diminished after the war ended, he changed roles and became an intelligence officer and later a staff specialist in Washington. He was eventually reassigned to his home state of Pennsylvania. He also became the manager of the U.S. Army Air Corps pistol team and developed into an expert with a Colt .45 handgun.

After leaving the military in 1968 as a major, Levy spent time working in the legal field as a clerk in the office of Judge Herbert Cain Jr. before finding his way into real estate. Along with two other brokers, he opened a real estate office on the corner of Broad Street and Erie Avenue in Philadelphia. He worked as an appraiser for banks and mortgage companies and stayed active in politics and local charities. At one point, he served on twenty-two different boards, including the United Way and the Philadelphia Federal Credit Union, and was one of the first African American members of the Philadelphia Board of Realtors. Sometime along the way, he met his wife, Miriam, to whom he was married for more than forty-five years. They had two daughters and three grandchildren.

James Williams left the army in 1946 as a first lieutenant and made his way to Muhlenburg College, where he was one of the first black men to attend. Always a diligent student, Williams recalled that his father had taught him that education is "the one thing they can never take from you." It enabled exceptionalism and success, despite all obstacles. This was a lesson that Williams always strove to live by and to pass along to his children. At Muhlenburg, he received his bachelor's degree and went on to Meharry Medical School from which he graduated in 1955. He had little money during medical school and often had to cook beans on the radiator to prepare his meals.

He began residency at Frankford Hospital in Philadelphia and after two years became a surgical resident at Mercy-Douglass Hospital, a historically black healthcare institution located in West Philadelphia. When he moved to Rebel Hill on Philadelphia's outskirts, Williams began to construct his own home, spending a considerable amount of time living in his own basement until it was finished. Seeking greater professional opportunity, he moved to Chicago to spend four years as a resident in pathology at Hines Veterans Hospital. Williams returned to Mercy-Douglass and became director of pathology in 1964 but found it difficult to find housing.

Williams eventually found a home for his family in a predominantly white neighborhood, much to the chagrin of his neighbors. Many walked past him without a greeting or turned away when he initiated conversation. One night, a neighbor imbibed too much alcohol and came to the front lawn yelling racial slurs. Williams told his children not to worry. He joked about bringing home a big German shepherd and naming it the slurs his neighbor used. The next time the man showed up and opened his mouth, the dog would come running. This was a personality trait he maintained for many years—humor in the face of racial tension. During his time as head of pathology at Mercy-Douglass, many patients came to him and expressed their relief at having a black doctor, as they felt comfortable that he would not perform any unnecessary experiments on them or abuse their trust because of their race. He was known by the staff as a personable man, speaking to hospital administrators and janitors with the same level of respect. He often made bets against Philadelphia sports teams to rile up his co-workers.

It was during this period that Williams reentered the military, joining the air force reserve. While enlisted, Williams worked at the air force base in Dover, Delaware, as a primary care physician. He spent six years in the reserves before retiring from the military for the second time in 1973—this time as a lieutenant colonel. Eventually, Williams became director of laboratories at John F. Kennedy Memorial Hospital in Philadelphia. He remained there from 1976 until the end of his career in 1991. He never made the kind of money many people assumed he made. He attributed this to being restricted from higher-paid positions because of his race. Williams raised his children without many material possessions but always provided what they needed. Often working out of his home and moonlighting in the emergency room to make ends meet, Williams was a busy man, but his children remember him always showing up for their games, at least for the few minutes he could spare.

Williams served as president of the Parent Teacher Association and as a scout master. He spoke proudly of his children to others but always told

A legacy long standing. *Philadelphia Chapter, Tuskegee Airmen.*

them they could do better to their faces. His son Bruce recalled that when he bought his first plane and received his flying license, his father did not act impressed. He was also involved with the local chapter of the NAACP and served as a mentor in a high school in northern Philadelphia. Following his retirement, Williams enjoyed going to air shows and reading books about flight. After learning to fly and receiving his wings in 1945, Williams did not fly a plane again until 1993 when his old friend and flight instructor, Roscoe Draper, insisted Williams join him. He obtained his pilot's license again in his early seventies but had to retire once again due to vision issues. His passions for flying and medicine remained throughout his life. He passed these passions to his children—two of his sons followed in his footsteps, one became a commercial pilot, and another became a doctor.

Despite the extensive training of the 477th Bombardment Group, and though some of its members attained multiple certifications for different types of planes, following their time in the military the members did not receive the opportunity to fly commercially. This meant that while serving, the men of the 477th Bombardment Group were unable to prove themselves as bombers in the field of combat, and after their service ended, they were not allowed to prove themselves as pilots back home. As such, the legacy of the Tuskegee bombers cannot be measured by the number of targets destroyed, the number of missions flown or the number of medals awarded. Instead, their legacy is built on their fight for equality within the military and their contributions to their communities following their time in the service. Returning to Philadelphia, these men became pillars of their community, dedicating themselves to the improvement of those around them. Serving as doctors, lawyers, brokers, educators and community organizers, their contributions to society did not cease when they left the military.

In examining this outstanding group of people, Americans must be able to look beyond one facet of their lives and see them as greater than just a few defining years in history. Their bravery was not limited to the air, their service was not limited to their enlistment, and their contribution to society was not limited to their symbolism as outstanding figures of the fight for civil rights. These were complex, complicated, imperfect men who show us that a lifetime is not defined by a single year, decade or title. It is measured in its totality. The Tuskegee bombers contributed a great deal not only to the city of Philadelphia but also to the world around them. They did not fly combat missions, drop bombs or destroy enemy targets, but the men of the 477th surely left their mark.

4

THE GROUND CREW BENEATH THEIR WINGS

The Mechanics of the Tuskegee Airmen

By Jeffrey Markland

The Tuskegee Airmen achieved highly distinguished service in the tour of duty during World War II. They were the first black combat aviators in United States history, and they had to deal with racist treatment and inferior hardware. Their legacy boasts a stellar combat record of enemy kills and successful escort missions. Unsurprisingly, much of the recognition stemming from their achievements has gone toward the pilots. They were in the thick of danger more than others, and they successfully completed the missions that made the unit so renowned. However, it has been easy to miss the fact that there were many more servicemen and women involved than just the pilots, and without their assistance, the missions would never have been flown in the first place. One particularly important group is the mechanics of the Tuskegee Airmen. Every plane required approximately ten technicians to keep it properly serviced and repaired so that that it would be combat ready. These technicians had to overcome the same racist obstacles as the pilots and had to work incessantly to keep old and obsolete aircraft in working order. The following chapter contains brief biographical sketches of three veteran mechanics: Private Cary Lee McCrae Sr., Staff Sergeant Elmer H. Wilson and Staff Sergeant Henry L. Moore. Although this barely scratches the service of the mechanics at large, the struggles and heroism of these three veterans provide a window into the essential service and sacrifice that kept the planes in the air.

Mr. Mac

Carey Lee McCrae Sr., known as "Kate" or "Mr. Mac" by his family and friends, was born to Calvin and Charity McCrae on February 15, 1925. He lived on Saybrook Avenue in Southwest Philadelphia and attended Bartram High School before joining the service. President Franklin D. Roosevelt signed Public Law 18 in 1939, which enabled black Americans to receive training for support services in the army air corps for the first time. At a lean build of five foot nine and 150 pounds, McCrae joined the corps as one of the youngest recruits.

In an interview from 1996, McCrae said he was the "baby" of the group, drafted at the age of eighteen. He was "young and gung-ho about being in the service." Although he said that he was drafted after graduating high school, his daughter, Jacqui, says he dropped out at age seventeen to enlist and lied about his age to do so. He "initially" had a sense of patriotism and "wanted to fight for America," hoping to prove that black Americans "loved their country enough to fight for it." McCrae completed basic training at Fort Meade in Maryland in the summer of 1943 and was sent to Keesler Air Force Base in Biloxi, Mississippi, to be trained as an airplane mechanic.

Private McCrae spent the remainder of 1943 at Keesler and graduated as part of its first class of black airplane mechanics in January 1944. By the autumn of 1943, Keesler housed more than seven thousand black personnel, including a small unit of mechanics from the Tuskegee Institute in Alabama. Conditions on the base were difficult, and they were occasionally plagued by severe weather. Jacqui says that when the river flooded "the building they were in floated," and they had to take refuge "on top of the building." But these hardships paled in comparison to what Carey called the racist "rude awakening" he experienced. He said that "they were very strict with the Jim Crow laws," and "the white officers didn't salute our black officers."

According to Jacqui, her father "talked about how they made him get off the train" or move to "a more uncomfortable part of the train" for the sake of "German prisoners of war." Watching the enemy receive better treatment than black servicemen instilled a sense of bitterness, especially considering Nazi Germany's racist and genocidal ideology. But the most egregious incident was the lynching of a black officer at the camp. A fellow serviceman "lynched him in the barracks" and left the body there for several days to "get the message across that they weren't supposed to get out of line." When Jacqui asked her dad about Keesler, she remembers that he angrily referred to it as "good old Biloxi."

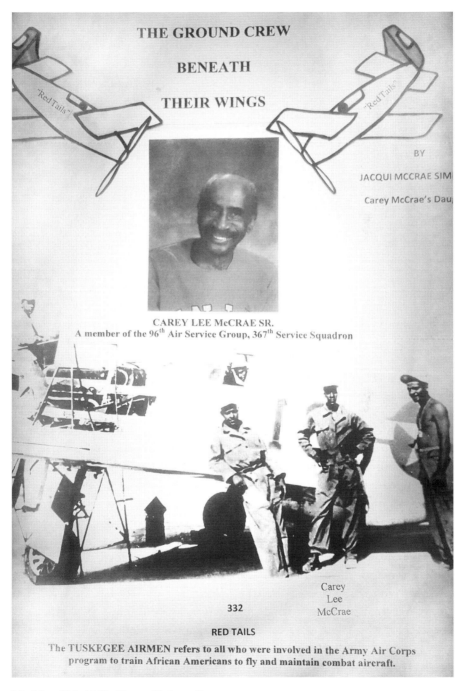

Mr. Mac. *Philadelphia Chapter, Tuskegee Airmen.*

Racism even permeated technical training. Mechanics at Keesler were taught to maintain and repair B-24 Liberator heavy bombers, but the black mechanics were forced to work with outdated and inferior hardware. According to McCrae, "The black airmen would get the older model planes such as the P39 and P37s which we called death traps or junkers." These were maintained by salvaging parts from decommissioned or scrapped aircraft. "We didn't have the best equipment, but we tried to do our best," he said. Despite the impracticality of forcing personnel to work with such equipment, McCrae and his companions were able to apply their training and creative know-how toward distinguished service. Instead of breaking their spirits, each act of disrespect motivated black soldiers to achieve a higher standard than attained by their white counterparts.

Private McCrae was assigned to the 332nd Fighter Group of the Tuskegee Airmen on December 25, 1943, and he departed for Italy on January 3. During his tour, he served as a mechanic with the 366th and 367th Service Squadrons of the 96th Service Group, which was attached to the 332nd Fighter Group. Initially stationed at the Montecorvino base near Salerno, McCrae witnessed the eruption of Mount Vesuvius, which lasted from March 17 to March 23 and destroyed several Italian villages, along with scores of American B-25 Bombers from the nearby 340th Bombardment Group. One can't help but wonder if he felt a sense of dread, especially after witnessing the Mississippi floods.

Whatever the case, the racism McCrae had experienced stateside continued in Italy. His enlistment record shows that he was issued a .30-caliber carbine rifle, but according to Jacqui, the black servicemen had their weapons "taken by the white officers." They were subsequently told that "they were not soldiers," but "professionals." They also had to continue using the clunky P-39 "junkers" until they received the more efficient P-47 in May 1944 and the P-51 Mustang—the finest fighter developed by the United States at that time—later that spring. By the summer of 1944, the 332nd had moved to a base near Ramitelli on the Adriatic coast, from which they flew combat and escort missions into the heart of the German Reich until the end of the war.

Private McCrae distinguished himself as an excellent mechanic during his tour. His sergeant and friend Edmund L. Wilkinson said, "We are the wind beneath the wings of the pilots." McCrae helped keep this strong and steady. On one occasion, his service squadron replaced an engine on the massive B-17 bomber, or "flying fortress." He recalled that his team was so skilled that the task was completed quickly, stating that "it took the white mechanics

Tuskegee ground crew in Ramitelli, Italy. *Library of Congress.*

a whole day to do what we accomplished in eight hours." Jacqui relates that on another occasion, an airborne B-24 Liberator bomber was damaged and "in distress," and when they landed at the airfield, the pilots were startled to see that the personnel were "all black."

The pilots "said it would take four days to repair the bomber," but McCrae and his team "did it in two." Working with a B-24 took some getting used to since they were initially accustomed to working the smaller P-37s. In one instance, Jacqui says her father managed to "get a laugh in" when he tested a B-24 by taking it down the runway where it "picked up speed and it went too fast" before landing in a ditch. This produced a four-day repair job.

Private McCrae was a skinny man, and this turned out to be a useful—albeit hazardous—asset for a mechanic. Sergeant Wilkinson later told Jacqui that her father was so slim that he was the only squad member capable of squeezing inside a plane's wings. This enabled him to become the designated mechanic for internal wing repairs. According to Jacqui, "They used to tie a rope to his foot so when he got stuck, they would pull him out." In one instance, he was badly cut and "got a gash on his hip."

Declassified documents from 1958 demonstrate that McCrae was involved in a secret mission in 1944, although it's unclear what that mission was. Considering his record and his willingness to put himself in harm's way, it's safe to say that he rose to the occasion. On another mission, in which they had to use a damaged plane, the pilots brought him onboard so that he could conduct temporary, on-the-spot repairs to hold everything together before the damage could be properly addressed.

Following the end of the war in Europe, Private McCrae arrived home on December 6 and was honorably discharged. Reflecting on his tour, he stated that "going to Italy was one of the best things that happened to me. Although we still faced racism, we were treated a little better." McCrae conducted himself with vigor, courage and determination, and he received a Good Conduct medal, a European–African–Middle Eastern Campaign medal (or EAME), a Victory medal and three Bronze Stars. He married his sweetheart, Mildred D. Harris, about a year and a half later and became a family man, eventually fathering four children.

McCrae hoped to make a career using his skills as a mechanic, but this turned out to be fruitless. He stated, "I tried to get a job as a mechanic, but they weren't hiring any blacks." One potential employer "told me filling out an application would be a waste of time because as soon as I left he was going to throw it in the trash." McCrae risked his life to serve his country and prove himself, but he was rewarded with racial oppression in his own home. After what he witnessed at the hands of racists in Biloxi, Italy and Philadelphia, his patriotism had all but slipped away, replaced by deep bitterness and resentment. According to Jacqui, it wasn't long before he pulled out a steel drum, dumped his uniform and medals inside and "poured gasoline on it and burned it up. He was just so angry." Private McCrae of the Ninety-Sixth Service Squadron would not utter a word about his service for another fifty years.

Since he couldn't find work as a mechanic, McCrae entered electrical school and graduated in 1948. He was subsequently hired by the electronics

Mr. Mac (*second from left*) and fellow bowlers. *Philadelphia Chapter, Tuskegee Airmen.*

firm Radio Corporation of America (RCA) and worked there for many years. He had learned Italian during the war, so RCA assigned him to the South Philly area where he worked as a television and radio repairman for the Italian community. Jacqui says that "people would be calling the house speaking Italian," and she or her sister would answer, saying, "Hold up, you want my dad." Their relationship with the Italian community was mixed, however, and Jacqui remembers how at baseball games some of them "would spit on us, throw popcorn, soda, and stuff down" from above.

After his career ended at RCA, McCrae took a supervisory role at Philadelphia's General Electric Space and Missile center, which he said was "one of the best jobs I ever had." Jacqui recalls seeing a picture of him in a white lab coat in a room containing a massive early-model computer. Despite his obvious talents, McCrae could not escape racial discrimination. According to Jacqui, GE refused to give him credit and compensation for his work stabilizing their rocket systems, which caused him to fall ill and suffer from ulcers. McCrae's work life was a difficult one, and Jacqui states that it was "always something racial" that made it so.

In 1995, McCrae volunteered for the AmeriCorps program at Barry Elementary School in Philadelphia to help children with reading comprehension. It happened that Jacqui was working there as the site manager, so they kept their relationship a secret to avoid the appearance of nepotism. She was his boss, and they pulled it off for a year and a half, calling each other Mr. Mac and Jac. She admitted he was her father upon hearing that he was involved in a bus accident during a field trip, but the principal decided to keep him on board as an aide since he was so popular with the students and faculty. Although he was in his seventies, McCrae attended AmeriCorps training programs and parties in which he would "dance his behind off," doing the "old-old head bop," as Jacqui's grandson called it. He was an entertaining man who always loved to dance.

The year 1995 ushered another important development into McCrae's life. Sergeant Wilkinson reached out to him and convinced him to speak about his service for the first time in fifty years. Only his wife, Mildred, had known about it. Jacqui relates how no one else had any idea, although her aunt, McCrae's sister, suspected he was involved with "something special." Wilkinson wanted the ground crews to be recognized for their service, so they spent time speaking at events and schools, from which McCrae saved a handful of thank-you letters from young students. In an interview from 1996, he said, "I found it a pleasure and an honor to serve with the Tuskegee Airmen." Wilkinson told Jacqui that her father was just as skinny as during the war. This was in spite of his insatiable appetite for Chinese food, which he ordered four times a week, according to his grandkids, Amber, Michael and Robert.

On February 27, 2000, McCrae was surprised to be presented with an honorable citation from the City Council of Philadelphia, delivered by Councilwoman Jannie Blackwell and her husband, the former U.S. congressman Lucien Blackwell. Upon receiving this "recognition of his distinguished service to his country," Jacqui recalls how it was "the first time I heard the man not be able to say anything," since he was "always running his mouth." Indeed, he was so touched that he was "lost for words." It certainly could not erase the anger he rightfully felt at the injustice he suffered throughout his life, but it is clear that this long-overdue appreciation was important to him.

Jacqui moved in with him during his last ten years. She says that they both had strong personalities, which caused them to butt heads often. He remained active despite his age and even climbed out the window—oxygen tank in tow—to fix his leaking roof. This concerned both his neighbors and Jacqui, who promptly phoned her brother. McCrae was mad that "people be running their mouths," but he agreed not to go back out on the roof. After

Mr. Mac and his students. *Philadelphia Chapter, Tuskegee Airmen.*

a disagreement, he bought a feast of Chinese food and left it on the counter for her, and when she went upstairs, she discovered that he had bought her a cable television subscription. This was his way of apologizing. When Jacqui's daughter and grandkids suffered from a severe California earthquake, he "made room for them in his home for a year or two."

Although McCrae might get angry and reveal a tendency to "go off on you," it was always clear that he was dedicated to supporting his loved ones. Carey McCrae suffered from emphysema in the last ten years of his life and from dementia in his final year. He died on May 17, 2012, at 11:51 p.m. He is fondly remembered by his loved ones, and Jacqui has worked very hard to maintain and share his memory. Without her project, which she titled "The Ground Crew Beneath Their Wings," this section on her father would not be possible, and the legacy of the Tuskegee Airmen would be robbed of the memory of a troubled yet gifted and steadfast veteran.

THE GOOD BARITONE (EVEN IF POORLY DRESSED)

Elmer H. Wilson was born on November 16, 1907, and grew up in North Philadelphia. He attended school up to the seventh grade and possessed a natural intelligence and technical savvy that served him throughout his life. As a young man, he worked as an auto mechanic for a local transportation company and occasionally drove some of their trucks. A lover of music, Elmer spent time singing in a barbershop quartet and joined the choir of the Dauphin Street Baptist Church. He developed a romantic relationship with the gifted pianist Mildred Johnson, who later described him as a "good baritone," who was "usually quiet and didn't have much to say." They spent time sharing their musical talents and going to boxing matches and football games. They came from religious families, and the couple attended church regularly.

In sharp contrast to the dignified Mildred, Elmer was notorious for his poor fashion standards. Johnson later told the *St. Petersburg Times* that he was "poorly dressed" when he asked her to marry him. She responded to his proposal by saying that she would think about it. Mildred's mother "saw a man of character disguised in pauper's clothing," so Mildred took her advice and agreed to marry him. They were wed in October 1941. Within four months, Elmer was drafted into the army air corps and started basic training at Fort Meade, Maryland, on February 26, 1942.

Elmer demonstrated his talents at Fort Meade. His natural intelligence and mechanical skill made him a prime pick for technical training at Moton Field in Tuskegee, Alabama. He wrote to Mildred, saying, "I'm going to some place called Tuskegee." He arrived in July 1942 and was distressed by the conditions on the base. Mildred recalled his letters in which he described their poor living conditions, stating that "nothing was prepared for them." Evidently, "the army did not plan for the Tuskegee Airmen to succeed." Furthermore, racial tension was high in Alabama. Black enlisted men from the North were keen to defend themselves when confronted with racism. This intensified the hostile reaction from some of the locals. Wilson kept his head down, staying on base and entertaining himself by watching basketball games.

Despite its unseemly appearance, standards of training and performance at Moton were exceptionally high. Elmer excelled with the hands-on work, but he occasionally struggled with the academic side of things. On one occasion, he was wrestling with the preparation for the mathematics portion of an exam. Mildred was intelligent and educated, so he sent her his coursework and phoned her for help. According to their daughter Debbie,

Elmer Wilson. *Philadelphia Chapter, Tuskegee Airmen.*

Mildred "broke it down for him and helped him," and he subsequently "took the test and aced it."

When a Tuskegee professor and his wife opened their home to Mildred, she took the train down and spent a month there while Elmer continued training. They attended church and basketball games during his free time, and he kissed her goodnight every evening before returning to the base. Mildred noted how the personnel at Moton "never looked happy." They remained "very quiet" and "somber." Mildred felt that this stemmed from the culture of the base. "It was like, 'why do we have to prove ourselves?' The white officers did not." Nevertheless, Wilson persevered and was made a technician for the Ninety-Ninth Fighter Squadron as a staff sergeant. He completed training in plane cameras and weaponry and departed for North Africa on April 16, 1943, and arrived on April 24.

During his two-and-a-half-year tour, Sergeant Wilson served in North Africa, Italy, France, Germany, Greece and the Balkans. According to his enlistment record, he "serviced and repaired" airplane machine guns and "repaired and serviced bomb racks and guns sights." He also "did loading of bombs and loaded machine guns." According to Debbie, he specialized as a camera technician. She recalls that Mildred would talk about how he helped develop "some kind of windshield wiper" for the airplane cameras, but he "never got credit for it." Debbie isn't certain if this is correct. Unfortunately, specific details about his time abroad are extremely sparse. He virtually never spoke of it, during the war or after. Mildred noted that "he sent me letters from Casablanca, Italy and Africa. He wrote 'love and kisses' all over them. He didn't write about the war or the racism they faced. Only that he couldn't wait to come home."

One gets the impression of a reluctant serviceman with an aching heart for his beloved wife. Nonetheless, Wilson distinguished himself during his tour. His service record shows that he received a Bronze Star medal, a Good Conduct medal and a European–African–Middle Eastern Campaign medal with nine bronze stars. He sent them home to Mildred in 1944, but they were lost in the mail. Mildred later said that before he arrived home in September 1945, he had discarded "everything, even his duffel bag. It was as if he was saying, 'I'm leaving all of this behind.' He just did what he had to do." All that was left were a few photos of himself in his uniform. Fortunately, one of the known anecdotes of his service is both noble and music related. Mildred said that "Elmer only spoke about the Italian children coming to camp." He loved how they sang with "beautiful tenor voices" and mentioned that he and his companions gave them "a lot of goodies" to take home.

Ninety-Ninth Fighter Squadron. *Philadelphia Chapter, Tuskegee Airmen.*

After the war, Elmer and Mildred settled into a large home in the Tioga-Nicetown neighborhood and eventually had two sons and two daughters. Wilson worked at Philadelphia Auto Parts in North Philadelphia and served as a supervisor until his retirement in 1974. His daughter Debbie says he was always working with his hands and "always fixing things." He had a work bench in their basement, and he "fixed people's toasters and appliances," as well as their televisions. Neighbors would approach him "on our block," saying, "Hey, Mr. Wilson" when they needed help. At home, he "remodeled our house," knocking a wall down to make "our living room bigger." He also "did the electrical work" and "arranged the fuse box" so that his children would understand how it worked.

Elmer and Mildred opened their spacious home to relatives when they needed a place to stay. Debbie says that they had "six bedrooms" and their third floor was "just like an apartment." She remembers various aunts and uncles "living in the house before they moved into their house." They "had a large family dinner every Thanksgiving" and decorated the place during the Christmas season. Debbie says her father was "avid about having that Christmas tree" and recalls how "every house on the block got a Christmas tree to put in front." They also hung lights but had to stop because "people would start stealing the lights." And they hung the American flag out front "every Fourth of July." Debbie believes her father was "bitter" about his military experience, but he was "still patriotic with that flag."

Debbie describes her father as "stern," "very disciplined" and "very regimented." If one of his children misbehaved, he "gave you the look. He didn't have to go much further than the look." He taught his children to make good use of their resources and local services like the public transportation system. He also "walked us a lot" and showed his children around the city. As his kids came up in school, he "helped us with science projects" and worked with his daughter Linda on a Morse code machine. Mildred was a Girl Scout leader, and she put her daughters through the Scouts. Elmer helped with their sleeping bags and taught them knots and other outdoor skills.

Elmer was an "avid reader." Every evening after work, he sat down with a "shot of gin" and "read the *Bulletin* and *Inquirer*" before supper. He loved movies about the Old West and was nicknamed "Mixie" after the cowboy actor Tom Mix. He was also a big baseball fan and would attend the Negro League games in Philadelphia. Debbie says he "did not like the Phillies because they were segregated," but he was a "big, big lover of the Brooklyn Dodgers" and a strong admirer of Jackie Robinson, the first black player in Major League Baseball.

Debbie describes her father as "a big lover of classical music" and a "big lover of Negro spirituals." He also played the ukulele and would sit on the porch singing "It Ain't Gonna Rain No More." Debbie says that old neighbors remember him for "fixing things" and for "playing the ukulele." He passed his love of music along to his children, and they all learned to play "the piano or some instrument at one time or another." Elmer also enjoyed having his son Mike play the saxophone with his band in their basement when they had nowhere else to practice. Debbie claims that the neighbors enjoyed listening in as well.

Another favorite pastime was "to go down to the Philadelphia airport and watch the planes go up." He would tell his kids that "they weren't like the planes back in Moton Field." This is all he would say to them about his service record. He was also a member at the Philadelphia Veterans of Foreign Wars (VFW) post no. 5943 and the American Legion post no. 968. Both Elmer and Mildred were also charter members of the Greater Philadelphia chapter of the Tuskegee Airmen.

In the early 1970s, Elmer suffered a stroke. This "devastated us," says Debbie. He "had to go to the VA hospital" for a pacemaker. Sadly, the procedure occurred close to Debbie's wedding in June 1971, and he was unable to give her away. She says that "my brother Tony gave me away instead, but the wedding party, the *whole* wedding party, went down to the naval hospital" to see him. "Tears came into his eyes" and he was "really appreciative of that." It was also around this time that his sons, Anthony and Michael, enlisted in the army and air force, which was something "that he was really pleased about."

In 1988, Elmer and Mildred moved to Tarpon Springs, Florida, where they lived out the rest of their lives. They joined the local American Legion post no. 10757 and attended Church of the Bayou Presbyterian (USA), where Debbie says his "voice bellowed" from the congregation as they sang. He still had "a very strong baritone." He also enjoyed watching the Phillies at Clearwater as they conducted spring training. Elmer and Mildred would "periodically" return to Philadelphia to visit their children and grandchildren during the holidays. Mildred had enjoyed Pennsylvania's snowy days, and Florida made her miss the seasons. Debbie says they would take the train since Elmer refused to fly; he still felt that they didn't make the planes like they used to and was "suspicious" about newer aircraft.

Elmer was known as Pop to his grandkids, and like every good grandfather, he would sneak them candy from time to time. Debbie was a health and physical education teacher and was strict about dental care, so she was upset when her kids told her that they "would get candy from Pop." She laughs about it now.

Elmer suffered from dementia in his final years. Mildred comforted him with her skills as a classical pianist. Debbie recalls that "in his later years when he was losing his memory, he would just sit there and listen to her." He loved to listen to Beethoven's *Moonlight Sonata*, which she played for him the night before he died. Elmer H. Wilson passed away on July 16, 1995, at the age of eighty-seven. He was lovingly remembered by his wife, children and grandchildren. Debbie says that he "lived a really full life."

About a year after Elmer's death, Mildred finally received replacement war medals for the ones lost in the mail in 1944. They were presented to her at a ceremony at the local VFW post with four surviving Tuskegee Airmen in attendance. Nick Contomarinos, the post commander, said, "I only wish we could have replaced the medals when he was alive." Mildred went on to give presentations about Elmer and the Tuskegee Airmen. After a speech in January 2009, she was approached by Congressman Gus Bilirakis, who asked her if she would like to receive the 2007 Congressional Gold Medal commemorating the Tuskegee Airmen on Elmer's behalf. At the acceptance ceremony in July, Bilirakis said, "The perseverance and courage exhibited by Staff Sergeant Wilson played an important role in the liberation of

Elmer Wilson. *Philadelphia Chapter, Tuskegee Airmen.*

millions of people. I am honored to have the opportunity to help recognize his intrepid service, as well as the support and resolve of his wife, Mildred, who served as a constant pillar of strength back home."

It is a shame that he did not live to witness the recognition that he deserved. Elmer never wished to go into detail about his war record, but thankfully his service to his country has not been forgotten. Because of Mildred's efforts, his family now possesses the medals honoring his hard work on behalf of the United States. Mildred passed away on April 16, 2014, at the age of ninety-four. This section on Staff Sergeant Wilson is indebted to her and her daughter Debbie, who was gracious enough to provide invaluable information about her father's life and character. They have ensured that the legacy of the Tuskegee Airmen includes the memory of this skilled mechanic, gifted baritone and dedicated family man.

DRAFTED WHILE OFF TO CANADA!

Henry Lincoln Moore was born in Ocilla, Georgia, to Andrew and Eliza Moore on April 8, 1921. His father was a reverend and a sharecropper, and his mother was a schoolteacher who always emphasized the importance of education. In an interview in the '90s with local military history enthusiast Ken Arnold, Moore recalled his shoeless walks to the segregated school approximately five miles away. This "fueled the frustration he felt" toward racial injustice in Depression-era Georgia. Despite these difficulties, his mother's emphasis on education stuck with Henry. He graduated as the valedictorian of Ocilla High School in 1940.

Moore drew inspiration from watching Taylorcraft L-2 "Grasshopper" planes. He "tried to get into the United States Army" to become a pilot but was told that they had "no work for Negroes." Other career opportunities were lacking, and a sympathetic woman working at the post office said, "Linc, there is nothing here in Georgia for you to do." He was fed up with segregation and racism and decided to move to Canada, but he was drafted into service while staying with a sister in Newark, New Jersey. Later, he claimed, "I ended up drafted in the United States Army against my will, on my way out of this country." The army sent Moore to drill at nearby Fort Dix, New Jersey, before sending him to Buckley Field, Colorado, in the autumn of 1942.

Once he arrived at Buckley, Moore knew that "we were going to be concerned with airplanes." He joined the Eighty-Sixth Aviation Squadron, a work squad consisting of newly recruited black personnel. They were assigned menial duties, including "policing the area," a euphemism for patrolling the base to clean up trash and "loose cartridges." Meanwhile, white cadets received pilot training. This only exacerbated the frustration felt among the members of the Eighty-Sixth. Fortunately, there were several sympathetic white officers who encouraged them to apply for any available opportunities.

Moore was very proactive and took "most of the tests offered." He later said that he "volunteered to play trumpet" and "to do everything under the sun." He also tested for aviation cadet training. Unfortunately, he didn't get into the band and he didn't hear a response regarding his aviation test (although he later learned that he passed). Finally, he passed a mechanics test in December 1942 and was sent to train at Lincoln Airbase in Lincoln, Nebraska.

Moore arrived in January 1943 and became part of the 789th Technical School Squadron. This was made of 250 black recruits and was the first all-black class of its kind. Major Fox, their commanding officer, told them, "You can make it, because you are better than anyone on this base." Moore recalled that they "treated us real raw." Racism existed on base and off. Moore refused to shop at the PX due to segregation, and several black squad members were denied service at restaurants and other shops in town. One restaurant manager "told two well-mannered and dressed soldiers that help was inclined to 'spit in the food.'" Nevertheless, the 789th bonded closely and worked hard. They "learned everything about 13 different aircraft" from "nose to tail, wingtip to wingtip." Moore emphasized how well "they could *teach* you" from scratch at Lincoln.

According to Ken Arnold, members of the 789th "caught on so quickly and proceeded from stage to stage, passing tests with the highest scores, that many instructors seemed to have been amazed." It turns out that due to racist screening practices, "these men had been selected at a much higher level of screening than were the white students." After graduation in the summer of 1943, the army sent Moore to Selfridge Field, Michigan. There he was assigned to the 302nd Fighter Squadron of the Tuskegee Airmen's 332nd Fighter Group. Moore volunteered to be a "crew chief," which carried the rank of staff sergeant and consisted of overseeing an aircraft's maintenance and clearing it for missions.

Moore told Arnold that "if I cannot fly the thing, I at least want to be the one in the cockpit, responsible for preflight inspection and day to day maintenance." Indeed, "the crew chief literally 'owned' the aircraft" and "the pilot just flew it." Sergeant Moore described their original commanding officer, Colonel Robert Selway, as "a racist" but noted that "he at least treated us militarily the way he had to do." Selway was replaced in October by Lieutenant Colonel (and later Colonel) Benjamin O. Davis Jr., who Moore said was "the first black officer I had over me."

Davis led the 99th Fighter Squadron in North Africa and quickly earned the respect and loyalty of his men. The 332nd was taken to Camp Patrick Henry, Virginia, in December to depart for Italy. The base nearly descended

(*From left*) Eugene Richardson, John Harrison, guest, Henry Moore and Aaron Witkins. *Philadelphia Chapter, Tuskegee Airmen.*

into chaos when the black personnel were barred from using the base theater and the officers' club, but Davis ordered his men to stand down so that they could disembark and begin their tour.

The 332nd shipped out on January 3, 1944, and Sergeant Moore recalled how "the convoy zigzagged and reversed course on many occasions to avoid the U-boats [Nazi Germany's submarines] that were still a threat." He also noted that "we thought on several occasions that we were being torpedoed when we heard explosions. The British escorts would drop depth charges and circle the convoy to protect us and on several occasions when the ship would plow into a 30 foot wave I thought we might not make it." When they arrived, Moore "kissed the ground" and felt free for "the first time in my life." They took to an airfield at Montecorvino, near Salerno, where Moore taxied P-39 Fighters in the winter rain.

The unit soon went to Capadochino Air Base near Naples, where they were upgraded with the newer P-47 Fighters and experienced the eruption of Mount Vesuvius, along with German bombing runs. Moore recalled that lava scorched several tents and that the bombings occurred at eleven o'clock every night. They were so consistent that "you could tell the time" by them. When the bombings subsided and the men had time off, they went to Naples and the surrounding villages and got along well with the residents. Many of the locals suffered from terrible poverty, which upset Moore and his companions. They decided to share their food and supplies, which they did in exchange for favors and chores. After their stay at Capadochino, the 332nd moved to the remote airbase at Ramitelli on the Adriatic coast, where they stayed for the rest of the war.

At Ramitelli, the Tuskegee Airmen received an excellent aircraft in the P-51 Mustang. Sergeant Moore recalled how he would "watch the P-47 and the P-38 pilots dogfight above the base, but when the P-51 came the P-38 and P-47 pilots wanted no part of them." The P-51 "was just too good as a combat fighter." Sadly, the transition to the newer aircraft witnessed the deaths of several of Moore's companions, including his pilot and closest friend. Moore became the crew chief of a B-25 Bomber and flew transport missions behind the front lines. He recalled, "I sat in the copilot's seat because quite often there'd be two of us in the plane going to pick up some people in rest camps." Their bomber was unarmed and was typically escorted by a P-51 since the Germans would "come down and shoot down anything they saw that was unarmed."

While stationed at Ramitelli, Colonel Davis granted Moore permission to return stateside to train as a pilot. He refused, however, as he wished to complete his tour as a crew chief. He loved the "hands on" experience with the aircraft, and the men under his command were skilled and successful mechanics. During his tour, Moore served with the 302nd, 99th and 100th Fighter Squadrons of the 332nd, and he organized the 332nd dance band and played the trumpet.

After the war, Sergeant Moore had no desire to return home, recalling that "I was not coming back to the United States." He tasted freedom in Italy and could not stomach returning home to racism and segregation. The Servicemen's Readjustment Act of 1944, or the GI Bill, changed his mind. He later said, "Mother always said that education will put you over the top and I thought here is the chance to get a college education." Moore returned with seven Battle Stars and Campaign medals and went to West Virginia State College, where he studied physics, mathematics and education. He also met his future wife, Mary Ion Ewell, while waiting in the registration line on campus. The two were married on September 8, 1951, and eventually had two daughters, Nadene and Meva. They moved into the West Mount Airy neighborhood of Philadelphia in 1960.

Moore continued pursuing education and received a master's degree in physics from Temple University and studied electrical engineering at Penn State and Drexel. For more than twenty years he enjoyed a lively career as a scientist for the U.S. Naval Air Material Center, the Frankford Arsenal and Diamond Ordinance Fuze Laboratories. He also served as an engineering supervisor at the U.S. Army Metrology and Calibration Center and worked on weapons development while employed at Frankford. From 1973 to 1983, Moore taught math and science at Roosevelt Middle School and then at Abraham Lincoln High School in Philadelphia.

Moore's daughter Nadene describes her father as a stalwart and brilliant man who was very active throughout his life. She says that "he would say he would do something and he would do it." He could always "figure out how to accomplish something." She remembers how a white neighbor refused to allow her family to use his pool. Moore built their own. Nadene also notes that growing up in West Mount Airy shielded her from much of the racism her father experienced. She recalls how her dad insisted on living peaceably and without bitterness. He told his daughters, "Don't be angry at white people, because it's not most of them, and we have good white people here."

Moore could "be a curmudgeon," but Nadene insists that "he loved his life." He would cook pancakes on the weekends and would have a fish fry on Fridays. He loved to listen to music from Gilbert and Sullivan operas with his daughters. He was an active member and an ordained elder at Summit Presbyterian Church, serving as the president of their deacons and trustees, singing in the church choir and playing the trumpet on occasion. Nadene recalls how the church gave him a key so he could keep an eye on the facilities and how he contributed to their church "clubhouse" parties. These constituted "the best times for that church."

For nearly four decades after the war, Henry Moore kept his service record under wraps. Nadene said that "we didn't even know he was a Tuskegee Airman" until "after he retired." When he started sharing his story, Moore sought to achieve the recognition that the ground crews deserved. Nadene describes her father and his veteran companion Dr. Eugene Richardson as "road dogs" who went on speaking tours "for a couple of years." They became like "rock stars" during Black History Month, Memorial Day, the Fourth of July and Veterans Day. Nadene taught at Martin Luther King Jr. High School in Philadelphia and was "*very* proud" to bring her class to witness her father speak in 2004.

In 2007, Moore attended the ceremony in Washington, D.C., in which the Tuskegee Airmen were presented with the prestigious Congressional Gold

Elmer Wilson. *Philadelphia Chapter, Tuskegee Airmen.*

Medal for their service. He was also invited to attend the inauguration of President Barack Obama in 2009 and brought Nadene and another Tuskegee Airman along. Nadene recalls how they were wearing their Tuskegee Airmen hats and were approached by thankful civilians at a rest stop. Moore also served with the Tuskegee Airmen International Organization, working on its board and serving as both the parliamentarian and president of their Philadelphia chapter.

Nadene describes her father as "strong willed and strong until the end," as well as physically and mentally fit right until his death. He continued to run errands and work around the house and was able to drive down to Ocilla for a family reunion in the last year of his life. On September 15, 2012, Moore was visiting a friend in Cheyney, Pennsylvania, and picking up supplies to bring home when he suffered a massive heart attack. Nadene has said how "he was waking up that morning and he was going to go to Cheyney and come back, and next thing we know we're in Roxborough Memorial Hospital and it's over."

Moore was ninety-one years old when he passed away. He is warmly remembered by his wife, daughters and two grandsons, among a host of other friends and family. This section on Henry Moore is based mostly on Ken Arnold's interview with Moore in the mid-1990s and a recent discussion with Nadene, both of whom deserve credit for carrying the legacy of this remarkable and unceasingly driven member of the Tuskegee Airmen.

These three sketches provide a small glimpse into the mechanics of the Tuskegee Airmen. However, the service, lives and characters of these three veterans deserve to be addressed in their own right because their service provides invaluable information on the struggles of the mechanics at large. They had to overcome racism at home and abroad while maintaining often inferior aircraft. They still found themselves in harm's way, even though they did not fly combat missions themselves. Without their service, the Tuskegee Experiment would have never been such a resounding success. For this reason, they deserve the recognition and honor befitting those who have dutifully served the United States.

5

ESSENTIAL ESCORTS
The Fighter Pilots of Tuskegee

Brandon Ray Langston

Naturally Submissive?

Former fighter pilot Dr. Eugene Richardson frequently speaks at various schools and universities to teach the public about the experiences and history of the Tuskegee Airmen. He persistently edifies his audiences about the spurious sophistry—and very existence—of the 1925 report out of the U.S. Army War College in Carlisle, Pennsylvania. After all, it is one of the most direct and proximal reasons the Tuskegee Experiment was necessary at all. The report, titled "The Use of Negro Manpower in War," took the most degrading contemporary ideas of white supremacy as a basis for United States policy on the inclusion and exclusion of black Americans in the military. The report treated a vastly diverse group of millions of individuals as a uniform collective—a blaring characteristic of racism. Their greatest commonalities were simply darker shades of skin and their treatment by white society on that basis.

This report is paramount to understanding the significance of the Tuskegee accomplishment because it encapsulates the racial pseudoscience of the time. Its claims include that blacks have brains ten ounces smaller than a European's, are inherently inferior in cognitive ability and moral character and are naturally subservient. Among other things, one could have asked why, if the alleged submissiveness was so natural, violent terror and coercion had always been necessary for its perpetuation. A respect for the truth was not held in high regard by the authors.

Dr. Eugene Richardson. *Philadelphia Chapter, Tuskegee Airmen.*

The report also states that blacks are far less courageous than their white counterparts. Touching on the use of black men as scouts, the report explained that "the negro is a rank coward in the dark. His fear of the unknown and unseen will prevent him from ever operating as an individual scout with success." The report concludes that black Americans ought to be judged by the same standards as whites but should also be restricted in their military opportunities, including opportunities to meet those standards. Due to their assumed lack of capability, the use of blacks in combat roles was still an experiment, so the overwhelming majority were relegated to noncombat roles. The report also decided that no black officer should ever be in command of a white serviceman of any rank. This assertion was central to military segregation through World War II. Every racial regulation stemmed from the belief that black people were inherently and irreconcilably inferior to whites.

DEGREES OF RACIAL SEGREGATION

Richardson and fellow fighter pilot William M. Cousins were unaware of this report's existence while they were members of the group that refuted its claims. Both men only learned the history and importance behind the

Tuskegee Experiment years after the fact. As a result, neither man understood at the time what they were a part of. American teenagers rarely payed much attention to politics, and it must be remembered that segregation was the norm. Cousins's daughter Leslie emphasizes this point with an often used but important cliché: "Those were the times." She explains that to better one's self, one understood the need to work within the construct of a racist society. This mirrors the belief of General Benjamin Davis Jr., the commander of the Tuskegee Airmen, that black people could most effectively work for their equality by proving themselves through their achievements, even if those achievements had to be made within the confines of segregation.

Richardson and Cousins came to represent Philadelphia in those achievements in different ways. Neither was born in the city. Cousins was born on July 21, 1923, in Goochland, Virginia, to Ruth and Samuel Cousins, but his family moved to Philadelphia when he was six. Richardson, on the other hand, was born in Cleveland, Ohio, on September 18, 1925, and spent his formative years in Toledo, Ohio, until 1943 when his family moved to Camden, New Jersey, when he was sixteen. Now just a stone's throw across the Delaware River from Philadelphia, he began to visit the city.

Both men grew up in the North, but their experiences with race were not identical. Cousins attended grade school at Michael Arnold Public School, which stood at Twenty-Second and Dauphin Street in Philadelphia until 1932. It was already integrated when he began classes in 1929, but a handful of other integrated schools converted to all-black schools during his years at Michael Arnold. This provided jobs for black educators because while white teachers could instruct black students, African Americans were prohibited from teaching whites. Even integration was unequal when it existed within an unescapable framework of segregation.

Richardson's experience was similar to that of Cousins for two reasons. First, de facto segregation existed in Ohio, but it was not state mandated. Second, his father, a minister whose job made the family move on occasion, made sure to live on the border between segregated and integrated communities. As a result, Richardson went to integrated schools through his vocational high school, "although there were darn few blacks there." Still, racism created boundaries between blacks and whites.

Many eateries near Richardson's home were open to everyone, but he and his siblings understood that certain places and parts of their town were off limits. Acknowledging it could have been a local myth, he remembers hearing of a restaurant that was purported to break the dishes of black customers after they left. Of course, colorism offered some exceptions. Richardson's dark-skinned sister had a friend with skin so light that she could pass as white. This allowed her to be served places where Richardson's sister could not. Black and white race relations sometimes had a prominent gray area.

Nothing clearly foreshadowed either man's membership in the air corps. Richardson had a fascination with planes since the age of five when he saw an air circus put on by black pilots but becoming a pilot himself, especially a military one, was a pipe dream until 1939. Previously, the army air corps had only white flying groups. Segregation necessarily forbade blacks from joining. After immense and persistent political pressure by the NAACP and other activists, President Franklin D. Roosevelt signed Public Law 18 in April 1939. This expanded the army air corps with the creation of the 99th Pursuit Squadron (later renamed the 99th Fighter Squadron), which became part of the 332nd Flying Group. It was an experimental flying group for black airmen. The air corps airworthiness directives also lowered the education requirement from a college degree to the ability to pass physical and academic tests regardless of official education. Cousins graduated from Central High School in 1941, but Richardson stopped his education after the tenth grade. The new eligibility requirements meant neither would be prevented from joining the air corps.

Neither Richardson nor Cousins were initially aware of the opportunity. They were typical teenagers and not politically mindful or active. They gave little mind to racism outside of their immediate experience. With the full force of the civil rights movement more than a decade away, racism was a despised but normal aspect of everyday life. Segregation was often navigated and rarely opposed in action. Until one is exposed to different ideas and ways of life, the status quo of one's native culture often feels normal because it is normal by definition. Even this is too simplistic, however. Incentives to deter people from changing their culture may be so aligned as to prevent such attempts, even when their possibility is realized. Even in the North, where the legal hand of Jim Crow did not reach, the consequences of obtuse resistance to the status quo could be severe enough to make any attempt seem futile before it was even made.

OFF TO WAR ON TWO FRONTS

Following Japan's attack on Pearl Harbor on December 7, 1941, Cousins knew his draft was imminent. He decided to join the air corps after a friend's mother told them that the newspaper said the air corps was taking black applicants. Richardson heard the same but in an unexpected way. After moving to Camden, teenage Richardson acquired a job with a jukebox company. He traveled to different venues with a white co-worker who collected the machine's nickels as Richardson cleaned the jukebox and changed records. One day in 1943, he and his co-worker, who was driving the car, were pulled over on their way to a venue. Along with the normal driving documentation, one's draft card was usually requested. The driver had his, but Richardson told the officer that he was seventeen and could not yet register. When he was eligible to register, he said, he wanted to be a pilot. The white officer "probably didn't see an inferior human being" but just a normal black kid. He told Richardson about a test at the customs house that would qualify him for flight school if he passed. Richardson later went to the custom house on Second and Chestnut Streets in Philadelphia and followed up on the officer's tip.

Cousins recalls that after passing the exams, white kids were given a reporting date a week later, but black kids had to wait much longer. Their applications had to go all the way through Washington, D.C., or so they were told. Richardson's application processed before his eighteenth birthday in 1943, which is when he would have had to register for the draft. He enlisted before he could be drafted and was sent to a classification center at Keesler Airfield outside of Biloxi, Mississippi. Conversely, Cousins was drafted while waiting for his air corps application to be processed. As a result, he had to take a second separate draft physical at Thirtieth and Market Streets. There he saw the same men who gave him the aviation cadet exam that he completed for the air corps application. They told him to go back to the draft board and say he was being called up the following Tuesday for aviation cadet training. When he did so, the board ignored him, and he was sent to Indiantown Gap, Pennsylvania.

Cousins managed to enter aviation training before long. While in Indiantown Gap, his experience as a butcher got him assigned to ration breakdowns. This was a sergeant's job, and it brought him more respectful treatment, but he was still just "a buck-ass private," he assures. Before long, he inquired about reassignment to aviation training and was told to get in touch with the Third Corps. He was unaware that his request was supposed to be sent through the chain of command and promptly wrote a letter to the general himself. Despite the chagrin of his officers, his request was granted and off he went to Keesler Field.

Cousins learned a little about the new black flying group he was joining from the country's largest black newspaper, the *Pittsburgh Courier*. The paper

William Cousins with his squad. *Philadelphia Chapter, Tuskegee Airmen.*

published many articles about the group and its significance to the paper's Double V campaign. Double V meant victory against racism and oppression, both abroad and at home (a double victory) during the Second World War. The movement was ignited by a letter published by the *Pittsburgh Courier* in January 1942, by a black American named James Thompson. Thompson implored that while sacrifices should be made for victory abroad, there was no reason not to achieve a second victory at home. Thompson's letter also brought up questions that black Americans nationwide wanted answered:

> *Should I sacrifice my life to live half American? Will things be better for the next generation in the peace to follow? Would it be demanding too much to demand full citizenship rights in exchange for the sacrificing of my life? Is the kind of America I know worth defending? Will America be a true and pure democracy after this war? Will Colored Americans suffer still the indignities that have been heaped upon them in the past? These and other questions need answering; I want to know, and I believe every colored American, who is thinking, wants to know. This may be the wrong time to broach such subjects, but haven't all good things obtained by men been secured through sacrifice during just such times of strife.*

Thompson went on to answer his own questions. He stated that America was worth fighting for and that changes would come but "not by any relaxation of the efforts to secure them." Thompson's reflective and pointed questions make one wonder if black servicemen had any reservations about risking their lives for their country. A country that largely treated blacks as an inferior subspecies of *Homo sapiens*, as the Army War College report claims they are. A country that denied them the supposedly sacred rights they went abroad to safeguard by the barrel of a gun. Reservations would be all too understandable, but both Cousins and Richardson did not think twice about it. When asked why he served, William emphasizes, "This is *my* country. It is the only country I know." Similarly, Richardson does not pause for a breath when asked if American hypocrisy gave him mixed feelings about serving. With simple honesty, he says that he was only doing what he believed was his duty. Though their country was dominated by white supremacy, it was *their* country. Equipped with this drive to fight, the two men went off to training.

Their army air corps training for the Tuskegee Airmen occurred largely in Mississippi, Alabama and South Carolina. The Deep South was much more uninviting and demanded greater caution. Richardson, of course, was well aware but did not allow himself to dwell on anxious thoughts. He was very fortunate to have a pleasant experience on the train ride down to his first stop for training in Biloxi, Mississippi. A white woman with her young daughter even kindly and with sincere curiosity asked about the aircraft ID cards he had. More remarkable was that he remained in his initial seat for the entire train ride. Normally when crossing the Mason-Dixon line into the South, black people were forced to the front train cars nearest the locomotive. There they endured the dirt, smoke and cinders that blew in through open windows from the laboring engine. Black passengers usually chose the lesser evil, sealing the windows and suffering the sweltering heat.

Biloxi, Mississippi, felt slightly alien. Cousins recalls that it felt less like home than Italy did during the war. The area itself is a beautiful place on the Gulf where white people sometimes went to vacation. Black servicemen were stationed in the corner of the airfield adjacent to the remains of a beach park that was off limits to everybody. Parts of Biloxi were off limits too, but only to Americans with brown skin. On one of his few excursions into town Cousins sought out the public library, which took him to the white part of town. A white police officer noticed this blatant transgression and promptly removed him from the area. The audacity of assuming a born and raised American citizen could use a public building in his own country was inexcusable and could not be changed by any amount of patriotic self-sacrifice. It could only be changed by white skin. The result of Biloxi's segregation was that Cousins never felt sure what he was and was not permitted to do.

After a brief stay in Biloxi, the next stop was the flying group's eponymous Army Airfield in Tuskegee, Alabama. There black instructors who were graduates of flight school programs that the government had instituted at a number of colleges taught them how to fly. The Tuskegee Institute, founded by Booker T. Washington in 1881, and today called Tuskegee University, was one such college. Richardson's memory of Tuskegee is painted by fair weather with clear skies, sweet smelling magnolias, a very routine cadet lifestyle and that the base was almost entirely black with the notable exception of Lieutenant Colonel Noel Parish. Parish was the third commander of the Tuskegee Army Airfield and is still fondly remembered with the same respect that he gave every one of his subordinates regardless of skin color. He ended the segregation instituted on the base by its second commander, Colonel Frederick von Kimble. The symbolism of that segregation is painfully representative of a theme pervading the Tuskegee Experiment's history. Among many wartime examples recorded in Benjamin O. Davis's autobiography was the fight black soldiers had to wage merely to obtain the opportunity to prove their equality. The illusion of a group's inferiority is easy to sustain when that group is denied the opportunity to demonstrate that the allegation is in fact illusory.

The surrounding town was less welcoming than the air base. The whites of Tuskegee, including a prominent judge and two government representatives, tried diligently to prevent the very construction of the air base. White locals also didn't want the black military police to carry guns (a necessary tool for enforcing their authority). Tuskegee's white sheriff shared this concern. Cousins's feelings about the sheriff are evident in the nickname he used for him at the time: Will "Shoot" Edwards. Decades later, Richardson returned to Tuskegee (without Cousins) for a convention with other former Airmen and was proud to see that they were ceremoniously met outside of town by a group of police that notably included multiple black officers.

The men first learned to fly at Tuskegee. Recalling first flights, Richardson exclaimed, "What a glorious day," and Cousins remembered this as "the greatest thing in the world." Still, he found it nerve-wracking when, from the back of the cockpit, his instructor told him seat to "take the stick." This type of pressure aimed to weed out those who would decide flying was not for them. He also got to fly with Charles Alfred "The Chief" Anderson. Anderson was the famous self-taught black aviator and chief aviation instructor who took Eleanor Roosevelt for a plane ride during her 1941 visit to the Tuskegee Institute. The First Lady was integral to the push for further black involvement in the military. This visit solidified her conviction that, as Richardson has said, "high levels of performance wasn't the province of guys with light skin."

Cousins laughs remembering one of his early flights when Chief Anderson was his check pilot. Anderson took him toward a stand of tall pine trees and said, "Give me some steep turns." He performed this stunt well, but on another occasion, Cousins was told (not by Anderson) that he didn't have "the intestinal fortitude" to become a pilot. He bet his critic a bottle of liquor and, upon completion of his training, was awarded both his wings and his whiskey.

The excitement of their first flights paled in comparison to their first solo flights. Richardson's was marked by respectful awe rather than outright exhilaration. To have such precise control over the plane was magnificent. It turned when he told it to or stayed straight if he pleased while carrying him through the sky. For Cousins, his first solo flight is remembered for its hilarity more than its visceral feeling. Landing after a practice flight, he looked to his instructor and "was wondering why he was getting out of the plane." His instructor stood on the wing and told Cousins to shoot him three landings. (Shooting a landing is when the plane comes in for a landing but doesn't slow down, so that it immediately takes off again.) "I wanted to pull him back in the plane" he said with a laugh. He was nervous.

The first two landings went smoothly but not the third. He grounded the plane, taxied across the unpaved runway to his instructor and hit the wind tee with one of his wings. As a civilian, his instructor had little authority to reprimand his carelessness, but he was later called into his major's office. He stood at attention for an hour, waiting to be scolded while the major worked at his desk. Cousins's relief must have been palpable when he was eventually told merely to "get the hell out of here." Cousins got off easy. Mistakes were normally met with harsh berating because in war any moment of negligence could kill a man or his fellow servicemen.

The rest of training went off without a hitch. Cousins and Richardson were awarded their wings, though not at the same time (Richardson wasn't awarded his until March 11, 1945). For Cousins, the ceremony was unceremonious. Rather than have the whole group in formation while an official pinned the wings on them, they gathered in the chapel and had family and friends pin them. Bitterness would be understandable, but the modest ceremony satisfied Cousins. Now a second lieutenant in the army air corps, Cousins returned home to Philadelphia "proud as a peacock" for his first leave in more than a year since leaving Indiantown Gap. He was joyously received by friends and family. Understandably, he planned to spend his limited time home seeing friends and dating girls. Still, he accepted an invitation to talk to students at his old school about his experiences in the army's first black flying squadron.

Leave ended before long and Cousins returned to Tuskegee to fly his first fighter plane, the P-40, and then went to Florida for gunnery training in the familiar AT-6 that he initially trained in. Firing live rounds for the first time, he shot at moving targets dragged through the sky by another plane. He was eventually sent to Walterboro, South Carolina, where a large, heavy plane called the P-47 Thunderbird awaited him. Less of an airborne chariot than gas-guzzling juggernaut, it could serve as much punishment as it could take.

In the previous century, South Carolina had produced one of the United States' most unapologetically proslavery statesman, John C. Calhoun, who gave a senate speech in 1837 arguing that slavery was a "positive good." Racial bigotry and dehumanization were open, and black South Carolinians generally needed their own institutions and businesses for group survival— from taxis to groceries to churches. It is therefore unsurprising that racial tensions were grimmer in South Carolina than in Alabama. Still, whatever the reason, Cousins never had any particularly humiliating experience there, at least on base. That was manageable despite being segregated. Outside the base's limits, caution proved especially necessary.

One weekend Cousins took a bus to Charleston, South Carolina, and was loaded on first because black folk had to sit in the back. Not long after, a small group of drunk white navy men were standing nearby, and one said to his buddy, in a voice purposely audible to Cousins, "God damn, a nigger lieutenant." Their chief was present and apologized to Cousins for his subordinate's comment. Cousins acknowledges that it could have been worse. If the navy man wasn't drunk or the chief hadn't apologized, then it would have indicated an acceptance for this obtuse and public racism directed toward an army officer. The offending sailor was not made to apologize though, and his confidence in making the comment at all speaks more than his superior's apology.

Richardson was in the class immediately behind Cousins and was never deployed to Europe. Cousins's class was the last one deployed as replacements for the 332nd Fighter Group, which was then flying missions out of the Ramitelli Air Base in Italy's east coast province of Campobasso. By the end of the war in Europe he'd flown fifteen missions, mostly escorting bombers. He was fortunate to never encounter an enemy plane, and his greatest

Tuskegee Airmen briefing in Ramitelli, Italy, in March 1945. Swarthmore's William E. "Porky" Rice is in third row. *Library of Congress.*

annoyance was escorting P-38s on photographic reconnaissance missions. "Those guys never wanted to come home," he said. "Always wanted one more picture, one more picture."

Italy did not keep Cousins long. The airmen had been training for the deployment to the Pacific until the atomic bombs were dropped on Japan in late August 1945. Neither Cousins nor Richardson remarked much about the dropping of the bomb except that it ended the Second World War. With Cousins's short war at an end, he was allowed to travel to Rome and Naples for a couple of days. The latter was quite beaten up by the time he arrived.

Some of the people he encountered had never seen a black man before and were very curious. Others had developed a distaste for black servicemen from the influence of occupying white troops.

Most Italians were welcoming to any visitor who brought food and supplies. Supplies were so short that they were asked to return their emptied bottles after drinking the Italian wine, which was improperly aged under the circumstances. Cousins had no complaints. He was soon sent back stateside where Richardson still was. The rest of their service stateside included flying when they could and being assigned to different jobs because there was now a surplus of military pilots. Both were discharged in 1946.

POSTWAR SERVICE

These Airmen's stories did not end with the war. After being discharged, both men went to Philadelphia to begin new lives. The increase in confidence gained during their service was particularly pronounced in Richardson. He hadn't completed school past the tenth grade but served alongside men much better educated than himself. He remembers one Airman was a teacher and another had spent some time at Cornell. Their increased confidence combined with the new opportunities brought on by the GI Bill allowed Cousins and Richardson to go to university.

While studying sociology at Temple University in Philadelphia, Cousins took a familiar job as a butcher. During this time, he met the woman whom he wed. Though years later they would separate, they had two children. Their son, Philip, was born first, followed by their daughter, Leslie, a couple years later. Leslie remembers that while growing up she did not know her father was a World War Two pilot. William Cousins wasn't hiding anything, he just rarely saw the need to mention his experience. The amusing result was that Leslie did not even know what a Tuskegee Airman was for many years.

Following his time at Temple, Cousins took some graduate classes at the University of Pennsylvania. One was a course in race relations that set the stage for the rest of his career. He took a job with the city of Philadelphia where his primary focus was fair housing. In 1961, he took a state-level job where, as director until 1965, he administered a law titled "Prohibition of Discrimination in the Selling, Leasing or Financing of Housing and Places of Public Accommodation." It was Pennsylvania's first fair housing law, and William Cousins brought it to fruition.

During this same time, in 1963, the famous March on Washington occurred and when Martin Luther King Jr. delivered his I Have a Dream speech. Cousins was not part of the march, but Richardson was present for that rapturous oration. He was in the crowd as Dr. King Jr. assured the nation in biblical language, simultaneously gentle and indomitable, that "we will not be satisfied until justice flows like waters, and righteousness like a mighty stream."

Cousins left his job in 1965 and took one with the predecessor to today's Department of Housing and Urban Development, then called the Housing and Finance Agency. His time at the federal level included nothing he feels fit to mention, but work wasn't his whole life. In the early 1970s, William Cousins was one of about twenty-five founding members of the Philadelphia chapter of the Tuskegee Airmen Incorporated.

This is where he and Richardson worked to ensure that the public could learn about the Tuskegee Airmen and their significance. Cousins had more time to devote when he left his federal job in 1981. "Have been retired and living the life since," he said. His retirement was largely consumed by gardening, reading and working at the local library. On May 14, 2014, William Cousins died at the age of ninety. His daughter, Leslie, remains involved in the Tuskegee Airmen Incorporated.

Richardson's postwar life was quite different from Cousins's. His first job after the service was selling cemetery plots. He called himself a "dead-end salesman." Needless to say, he did not see it as a permanent position. Education in math and science was abundant and necessary during pilot training, so he decided to teach those subjects at the middle school level. A college degree was needed to be a substitute, so after acquiring a degree, he was called in to Barratt Junior High School at 1599 Wharton Street in Philadelphia. He enjoyed teaching so much that he decided to become certified and acquired a full-time position at Barratt.

This was in the 1960s. The superintendent, a man named Mark Shed, wanted to promote integration in Philadelphia schools and asked for volunteers to transfer to schools in the white section of northeastern Philadelphia. Richardson was one of those teachers, and so he went. He happily recalls very little trouble at the school. "The kids take you as you are," he explains, and though some faculty were resentful, the school principal was on board with the program. This meant opposition would not be tolerated, and he was generally treated with respect. In fact, Eugene Richardson and the principal, Walter Scott, became friends and fishing buddies during his time there.

After the success of this program, the same superintendent, Mr. Shed, wanted to further integrate the staff and pushed Richardson to become a principal. Richardson decided to do just that and went to Pennsylvania State University for his principal certification. He spent the rest of his career as a middle school principal in Philadelphia. In total, he spent thirty-five years in the Philadelphia school system before retiring in 1991.

As a member of the Philadelphia chapter of the Tuskegee Airmen, Richardson spent an impressive amount of time researching the group's history and devotes a large portion of his time to the organization as one of their main educators. Since becoming a spokesman for the chapter, he has often traveled to schools and other events to speak about the history and significance of the Tuskegee Airmen. He also advocates for the organization's scholarship fund. The scholarship is awarded yearly to students of all skin colors.

To his young audiences Richardson emphasizes the primacy of an honest and resilient character in overcoming obstacles. Obstacles are certain to come to all individuals and societies, so this theme never dies, it only manifests itself through different stories. Richardson is also adamant that while the Tuskegee Airmen hold a special significance to black Americans, they ought to be role models for everyone. This message is central to the mission of Find Your Wings, the organization that his wife, Dr. Helen Richardson, founded to help young Americans discover their talents, capabilities and passions.

William Cousins and Eugene Richardson both partook in the Tuskegee Experiment and therefore hold a level of responsibility for the accomplishments of that group. Their refutation of official racial beliefs about blacks led directly to President Harry Truman's Executive Order No. 9981 that officially ended all segregation within the armed forces in 1948. Dr. Richardson witnessed other national milestones too, like Dr. King's famous speech and President Barack Obama's inauguration (which Leslie attended in her father's stead, though she is unsure why he did not wish to go). He was also present with William Cousins when the Tuskegee Airmen were awarded the Congressional Gold Medal in 2006 for, as the medal states, "Outstanding Combat Record/ Inspired Revolutionary Reform in the Armed Forces."

This revolutionary reform constituted President Harry S. Truman's executive order, which allowed for various unprecedented military accomplishments. While the 1925 War College report stated that no black officer ought to have authority over any white serviceman, Truman's order for desegregation allowed Daniel "Chappy" James (another Tuskegee

Tuskegee Airman Dr. Eugene Richardson. *Philadelphia Chapter, Tuskegee Airmen.*

Airman) to become a four-star general; Benjamin Davis to retire as a three-star general (awarded a fourth by President Bill Clinton); and Michelle Howard to become the first female four-star navy admiral, white or black. Howard retired in 2017. While the gold medal is a source of pride, it was as long overdue as the general recognition of all that those from Tuskegee achieved. Leslie notes with hope that their story is now being told more widely and their legacy will be understood.

Richardson and Cousins served their country during the war and their city after it. The contribution of the Tuskegee Airmen to equal rights is unappreciated because it is not grasped by most people. Neither Richardson nor Cousins even saw many black teachers growing up, which signals why Richardson took such immense pride when former president Barack Obama said that he stood on the shoulders of the Tuskegee Airmen. Neither man believed they would live to see a black man become the president of the United States. There was never a reason to believe they would, but there was every reason to believe they wouldn't.

There was no grand idea of postwar equality consciously motivating Cousins's or Richardson's service. They seized opportunities that inevitably promoted a less racist society. The Tuskegee Airmen were not *merely* the first all-black air corps group, they were the refutation of the justification for oppressing black Americans in the military and, by extension, society. Most of the airmen were unaware of the 1925 War College report, but they knew its ideas existed because they were directly affected by them every day. To say they were motivated by patriotism might ostensibly border on the type of romantic aggrandizement that is the staple of most American military stories, but it is the simple truth. The unfortunate but important irony is that they fought against oppression in the name of a country that oppressed them. They made clear that people with dark skin and African ancestry were, it turned out, able to fly airplanes in combat with extraordinary skill, courage and reliability. So reliable, in fact, that their services were often requested by white bombing units for escorting bombing raids over Europe. The 1925 report was wrong on all its charges. Even in the dark, the "rank coward" was nowhere to be found.

6

NECESSARY MEDICINE

Medical Care and Experimentation at Tuskegee

By Matthew Rothfuss

When one remembers the Tuskegee Airmen, visions of proud pilots permeate the mind. Red tails of heroic battle stories and Hollywood film, the Airmen exist within a specific place of World War II and African American history. Their deeds and their service should never be forgotten or underscored. The pilots, however, remain only a single component of the large number of men and women who trained in Tuskegee, Alabama, and served this country in World War II. A large support system was in place, including a medical staff with trained nurses serving in the Army Nurse Corps (ANC) and a group of nurses studying at the Tuskegee Institute.

NURSING AT TUSKEGEE

These nurses were given a chance to serve by a large tide of growing sentiment among people in positions of leadership, such as Eleanor Roosevelt, and by African American individuals who successfully petitioned for the opportunity to serve, like Della H. Raney. Approximately twenty-nine accredited nurses served during the course of the war at Tuskegee, while many others enrolled at the nursing school at the Tuskegee Institute and aided the medical staff both directly and indirectly.

Through online sites such as the Tuskegee Army Nurses Projects, many stories about these nurses are accessible. Perhaps most famously, individuals like Della Hayden Raney (1912–1987) paved the way for black women in the armed forces. After pleading her case with the Army Nurse Corps and the

Deployed nurses, including Philadelphia's Catherine L. Harris (*front row, third from left*). *Library of Congress.*

American Red Cross, Raney was the first African American accepted into the ANC in April 1941. Maw Raney, as she was known to her fellow nurses, was a professionally trained nurse who graduated from the Lincoln Hospital School of Nursing in Durham, North Carolina. This school was the first of its kind to accept African American students. Raney was commissioned as a second lieutenant in the ANC in 1941 and was stationed at Fort Bragg as the head of black nurses there.

By the following year, the army had transferred Raney to Tuskegee Army Airfield in Tuskegee, Alabama, and she became principal chief nurse with a new rank of first lieutenant. She eventually gained the rank of major and received several medals, going on to a meritorious career in the army before retiring in 1978. The National Black Nurses Association and the Tuskegee Airmen Foundation jointly started a scholarship in her name in 2012. The Della H. Raney Nursing Scholarship awards a $2,000 annual scholarship to women seeking a bachelor of science in nursing and who have achieved at least sophomore status.

Another nurse, Second Lieutenant Norma Greene, was also one of the earliest nurses at Tuskegee. In addition to her admirable service record, Greene's actions on one fall day in 1942 perhaps foretold later civil rights activism in the area. According to the Saturday, September 26, 1942 edition of the *Pittsburgh Gazette*, Greene was riding a bus to Montgomery, Alabama, from the base when she was presumably asked to vacate her seat by the bus driver. Ensuing reports differ about what exactly happened, but the young nurse was arrested by local police and detained for several hours before eventually being released.

After local authorities realized she was military personnel, they dropped all charges (Greene was out of uniform on a Saturday shopping trip). Alan M. Osur's book *Blacks in the Army Air Forces During World War II*, which was compiled using interviews of Airmen and letters of correspondence, claims Greene was beaten by police after refusing to get off the bus as ordered by the driver.

First Lady Eleanor Roosevelt was also supportive of the efforts at Tuskegee. Known as an advocate for civil rights, and for expressing her thoughts in a column called My Day, Roosevelt championed equal opportunity and often publicly denounced actions she saw as detrimental to African Americans. One example came on February 27, 1939, when she announced in My Day that she was resigning from the Daughters of the American Revolution (DAR). This action, coming after the organization refused to give permission to black singer Marian Anderson, made national headlines for its implication for race relations in the United States.

In 1940, Roosevelt published *A Moral Basis for Democracy*, arguing that ethical responsibility to fellow citizens and equality of rights are essential in a healthy democracy. By 1941, Roosevelt was more involved in race relations and visited Tuskegee, Alabama, in the spring. Much writing exists about her April 1941 trip to Tuskegee, particularly her trip up in an airplane with African American pilot C. Alfred "Chief" Anderson. Still, accounts generally neglect to mention that the first lady also visited other facilities at Tuskegee, including the newly built three-story Infantile Paralysis Center.

Roosevelt inspected the facilities that had recently been tasked with combating infant paralysis by the newly formed National Foundation for Infantile Paralysis. Now called the March of Dimes, this was created in 1938 by President Franklin D. Roosevelt as an attempt to alleviate the conditions of and find a cure for polio, a condition with which Roosevelt had been diagnosed in 1921. In 1939, President Roosevelt visited Tuskegee, where he visited the veterans hospital and met with several key figures to help facilitate the foundation's vision for a new hospital built specifically to research polio's cause.

Although these three figures represent the growing changes within both the country and the armed forces and provide examples of the tumultuous times in the 1940s, their stories are widely accessible. However, one individual whose fascinating life and service to this country has not been told is that of Miss Alma Elizabeth Bailey. Her story is of a small-town girl—a gifted singer and neighborhood nurse, a dedicated student with a no-nonsense approach to her patients, a loyal employee who found success and a cherished community and church member. Her perseverance and dedication to service has traveled with her, and her connection to Tuskegee and its integral place in our country's history honors our past.

PATH TO TUSKEGEE

Miss Alma Elizabeth Bailey was born in the small town of Middleburg, Kentucky, in 1925 to a family of seven children, including her twin. Her parents, both educated, instilled in her a strong sense of pride and a drive to accomplish. Still, Miss Bailey grew up in a poor household, and while her small hometown was largely integrated, she still attended all-black schools. As a child she played nurse for her family and friends. Miss Bailey recalls "patching up the neighborhood" wherever she went. Besides an affinity toward nursing, Miss Bailey had other talents. At an early age, she began to learn how to play the organ and piano in hopes of a musical career.

Since it was largely discouraged for left-handers to play the organ at the time; however, Miss Bailey ultimately gave up lessons to focus on singing. Miss Bailey excelled at singing and joined the church choir at her Baptist church, ultimately becoming its lead singer. As she grew older, she dreamed of a music career, with a great desire to become an opera singer. Almost everyone in her community and family still thought she should go into nursing. At one point her mother advised that "Uncle Sam needs nurses not opera singers."

Two external factors would conspire to send Miss Bailey on a career path toward nurse instead of opera singer. First, the United States entered World War II in December 1941, creating a need for nurses within the armed forces. Second, the Nurse Training Act of 1943 (or the Bolton Act) was passed in the spring of 1943 to combat the shortage of ably trained nurses

Nurse Alma Bailey. *Philadelphia Chapter, Tuskegee Airmen.*

serving in the war. Among its provisions, this law set aside money to create a program to send qualified young women to accredited nursing schools across the country. This program was named the United States Cadet Nurse Corps (UNC) and was created in July 1943.

The program consisted of an intensive thirty-month nursing program (compressed from the usual thirty-six-month program) designed to train young women between the ages of seventeen and thirty-five who had graduated from an accredited high school and were in good health. The UNC came to provide money to more than one thousand nursing schools across the country for accelerated nursing programs, and through the efforts of organizations like the NAACP and individuals like First Lady Eleanor Roosevelt, it also included black colleges such as the Tuskegee Institute.

According to Miss Bailey, right after she finished high school in the summer of 1943, there was an announcement about a certain number of scholarships for young women from the United States Cadet Nurse Corps. She remembers that only the white schools in the area were notified or offered paperwork from the UNC directly. Luckily, the UNC information was widely covered by many media outlets. Moreover, several teachers from Miss Bailey's school knew of both the Tuskegee Airman and the UNC scholarships and communicated with the mothers in the town.

As a result, several black mothers approached the superintendent of the white school to inquire about the UNC and request more information. Eventually, ten young black women from the area were accepted into the program. Miss Bailey was selected due to her good grades and promise as a young nurse. In September 1943, only a few months after Miss Bailey had finished high school, she traveled to Tuskegee, Alabama, to study nursing at the Tuskegee Institute under the provision of the UNC. Miss Bailey was only seventeen, and it was her first trip to the Deep South.

RESTRICTIONS OF RACISM

The students rode to Tuskegee on the Tuskegee Railroad, arriving at the Chehaw Train Station. Known then for its Civil War significance, traveling on this railroad must have been monumental for a young person such as Miss Bailey. When she arrived in Tuskegee, it was like stepping into another world, an altogether different part of America she had only heard about. She grew up in small-town Kentucky with segregated schools and racial tensions, but nothing prepared her for what she called the "farther south."

Miss Bailey explains that she came from a far more integrated residential community than what she experienced in Alabama, and when she arrived in Tuskegee, she discovered it was totally segregated. She adds that when she and her fellow students arrived at Tuskegee, they were shocked at the gated nature of the Tuskegee campus and its restrictions.

At the Tuskegee Institute, Miss Bailey and another young woman she knew from Kentucky shared a dormitory with four other students. Miss Bailey explains the living situation was at odds with the idyllic childhood and freedom she experienced earlier in her life. The students were forbidden to travel alone off campus and were only allowed to leave in small groups under strict guidelines. They were warned of potential horrors that could befall young women outside of the protection of the campus. Surely, the case of Norma Green remained paramount in their minds.

Norma Green, a Tuskegee nurse, volunteered for overseas service in 1942. In preparation for her trip abroad, she took a trip shop to Montgomery, Alabama. When she boarded the bus to return to Tuskegee, the driver refused to drive her and called the police. When the police arrived, they arrested her and proceeded to treat her badly. They beat her on the way to the station, doused her with whiskey and stole her money. They dropped the disorderly conduct charges they filed against her after learning of her work as a nurse for the U.S. Army.

Some of Miss Bailey's classmates, women from states like Massachusetts, California and New York, were especially shocked at the strict regulations, as they were accustomed to possessing relative freedom to travel wherever and whenever they pleased. Miss Bailey remembers feeling scared of leaving the campus. Downtown Tuskegee, which was a few miles walk from Miss Bailey's dormitory, was only accessible if the students traveled in a large group and compensated well for daylight hours. Fortunately for Miss Bailey, there existed a sort of makeshift bazaar across from the campus with temporary stores lined up across from the gate. These places opened most days. Still, even visiting these required a chaperone. Miss Bailey describes it as a constant state of "never [being] allowed to go anywhere alone."

Miss Bailey's schooling was a mix of training at the John A. Andrew Memorial Hospital at the Tuskegee Institute, visitations to the local veterans' hospital and classes on campus. The UNC provided her with her own personal nursing capes and a uniform. The uniform consisted of a cap, bib, black stockings and white shoes. She was also given books and all meals were provided for at the cafeteria. Miss Bailey describes her daily experience as an incredible amount of walking, what with the back and forth from the cafeteria, classes, hospital and dorms.

Per dormitory rules, students were required to sign in and sign out every time they left and had house mothers who monitored their bedtime and daily activities closely. Another aspect of the program was the requirement that all students had to go to church on Sundays. Miss Bailey reminisces that she and other students would climb under their beds some days to hide from their house mother. As students were required to sign in to church, those reluctant to attend arranged for fellow students sign in for them.

The UNC program also provided students with benefits. Not only did Miss Bailey receive a top-notch nursing education, but she was also paid twenty dollars a month for the first year she was in the program. This increased to thirty dollars a month for the second year. She also loved helping people and saw this as a great way to serve the country.

A QUIET EXPERIMENT

While she was a student at the Tuskegee Institute Nursing School, Miss Bailey was assigned the B Ward at the John A. Andrew Memorial Hospital, which was originally established in 1892 as the Tuskegee Institute Hospital and Nurse Training School. In 1913, it was remodeled and renamed after a large donation in honor of a trustee's grandfather. By World War II, it was regarded as the best hospital for black patients in Alabama. It was also the site of the Tuskegee Study of Untreated Syphilis in the African American, a forty-year initiative by the U.S. Public Health Service.

This study, made public in 1972 by health service employee Peter Buxtun, is arguably the most infamous and unethical public study in U.S. History. Study organizers at the Public Health Service reasoned that African American men in Macon County, Alabama, due to the area's poverty and poor educational system, would neither seek treatment nor respond to sexual education. They rationalized the study as scientific research that did its participants no harm.

Some six hundred men participated in the study, many of whom contracted syphilis prior to the study and remained untreated (even after the discovered applicability of penicillin in 1947). This often led them to pass the disease to spouses and even some offspring. At the hospital, young Alma Bailey, unknowingly at the time, was involved in this Tuskegee Experiment as a student with the UNC at Tuskegee.

Assigned to the B Ward, which had about eight patients infected with syphilis, Miss Bailey remembers the worst patient was Mr. Brown. She describes his physical condition as "so eaten up by the syphilis that he didn't even have a penis." One of her main responsibilities was to speak to the patients and take notes. Miss Bailey remembers one day when taking care of an especially sick patient, she stuck her hand on a safety pin. She worried she was going to contract the disease and die.

Miss Bailey recalls Mr. Brown and the other patients as very nice. Many years later, Miss Bailey remains emotional discussing this experience. She explains with a heavy heart that she didn't know at the time that her patients represented "guinea pigs." She only realized this proved the case six decades later when it became public that these men were tricked into the study. The study recruited patients by offering them free treatment. It only delivered placebos and required all patients to consent to an autopsy in exchange for funeral benefits.

When remembering those years, Miss Bailey also notes her disappointment that she did not serve in the armed forces directly or at the Tuskegee Airfield with the Tuskegee Airmen. In addition to her duties at the John A. Andrew Memorial Hospital, Miss Bailey worked at the local veterans' hospital where many Tuskegee Airmen had been transferred. This allowed her to help treat black soldiers who suffered from posttraumatic mental conditions. The large hospital was segregated, and Miss Bailey was assigned to the psychiatric buildings.

BATTLE FATIGUE AND ITS HIDDEN DANGER

Miss Bailey describes that the buildings of the veterans' hospital were numbered from A–Z, with later alphabet letters such as R or S designating worse conditions, such as schizophrenia. All her patients were black men who had come back from the war. Many suffered from paranoia and occupied a variety of mental states. Miss Bailey recalls the conditions that they experienced as ranging from tremors, mumbling, paranoia, schizophrenia or fear, with patients displaying signs ranging from typical to psychotic.

At that time, post-traumatic stress disorder (PTSD) remained a condition undiagnosed by the psychiatric profession. It was only recognized in 1980, thirty-five years after the Second World War concluded. While military authorities recognized mental states in soldiers that they identified as "battle fatigue" and "shell shock," the consensus held that these corresponded with weakness. There existed no limited tours of duty for Americans who fought in World War II. Military culture embraced the idea that the more combat one saw, the better one adapted.

Units that experienced combat early in the war remained in the war. The First Infantry Division, for example, experienced more than three hundred days of combat, beginning in November 1942, and concluding with the collapse of Nazi Germany. While psychological casualties constituted about 30 percent of America's total, broken soldiers received treatments devised during World War I. Aversion therapy—forcing soldiers to face their expressed fears—sought to shock patients into returning to the front. Sometimes military officials took things into their own hands, rooted in their own code of machismo.

Famously, U.S. army general George S. Patton called two soldiers cowards and slapped them in 1943. While Patton received his own slap on the wrist from his superior, U.S. army general Dwight D. Eisenhower, this proved a public relations maneuver. Patton led Operation Fortitude, an important decoy mission to confuse Nazi Germany about the location of the Allied

General George S. Patton meeting with Bob Hope days after slapping soldiers. *Library of Congress.*

invasion of Europe, or D-Day. Once American forces landed on the continent, Patton resumed combat command.

In a case even more extreme, U.S. army private Edward Donald Slovik received the death sentence for his refusal to participate in the Battle of the Bulge—a counteroffensive mounted by Nazi Germany against the Allies in the winter of 1944—due to his overwhelming fear of combat. Slovik died by firing squad on January 31, 1945. Authorities buried Slovik in France, in plot E of the Oise-Aisne American Cemetery in Fère-en-Tardenois. His grave, lacking a name, resides among ninety-five American soldiers executed for murder or rape.

This served as the context for Alma Bailey's work treating Tuskegee Airmen who returned stateside due to psychological breakdowns. Every day, Miss Bailey received assignment to the hospital and checked on her patients. She acknowledges the archaic approaches, noting that she and her colleagues lacked modern medicine. But they did the best they could. This is echoed by Tuskegee nurse Irma Dryden.

The humiliation Dryden suffered as an African American woman serving her country while being forced to dine behind a curtain on a train to avoid upsetting white passengers gave her strength. According to Dryden, in an interview with CNN, "I knew I could give them strength, and I did." Perhaps more than anything, Miss Bailey, Dryden and the other Tuskegee nurses offered the men of Tuskegee necessary "moral support."

They required this. One of the ghastly procedures for treating "combat fatigue" involved placing electrodes on either side of the head. This severely shocked patients. They foamed at the mouth and remained unconscious all day. The atmosphere was tense, loud and often violent, and the female nurses were on constant alert. Some of the hospitalized men would even try to rape the nurses. Several of the nurses Miss Bailey knew were raped. Miss Bailey described a specific incident when a man tried to rape her.

Miss Bailey entered one of the buildings during a routine shift and there were about seventy men in a room in robes. All of their heads were shaved. Her duty was to take their temperatures. While she was taking one patient's temperature, another jumped on her back and threw her on the bed. But Alma Bailey was "tough"; she grew up with a brother and they used to climb trees together. She knew how to fight back, and she had a foot ruler in her bib apron. When the man came at her, she pulled the ruler out and "popped him" hard with it. He leapt away in pain. She chased him, hitting him over and over.

The rest of the patients thought it was funny and were clapping at the scene. Miss Bailey followed the culprit to the exit where some hospital attendants finally interceded. According to Miss Bailey, five black male attendants were supposed to be in the building, stationed every ten beds or so. Yet if a nurse did not date one of the attendants, they offered no protection. Miss Bailey refused to date them. Miss Bailey remarked, "They are attendants and you are a nurse—why would you date attendants?" On that day, the attendants stood outside the building instead of protecting her. She protected herself.

BECOMING A NURSE AGAIN

Miss Bailey's nursing school class had a total of fifty-six students. Starting in September 1943, the class was almost two years into the program and close to finishing when the war ended. Miss Bailey was at Tuskegee from 1943 to 1945 but was on leave when the war ended. Although the UNC ended in 1948, and all classes were permitted to finish, Miss Bailey remembers being notified that the scholarship program was disbanded while she was on leave.

At that point, if she was going to go back and finish her nursing school at the base, she would have to pay.

For Miss Bailey, this was not possible. She was one of seven children and her family had no money. Unfortunately, this meant the end of Miss Bailey's UNC experience. The origins of the decision to charge students remains a mystery. However, Miss Bailey ultimately succeeded in becoming a nurse despite this apparent setback to her career ambition.

Back in Middleburg, Kentucky, Miss Bailey wondered what her next step should be. Her experience and quick thinking enabled her to move with the career she started at Tuskegee. As she recalls, one of the white surgeon's black maids at the local hospital had a large tumor. The hospital was segregated, and all black patients were placed in two rooms in the basement next to the furnace room. Because of the segregation, most of the white nurses only worked upstairs.

This situation, segregated health care, remained common in the South, even after the passage of the Civil Rights Act in 1964. It did not begin to change until the following year with the enactment of Medicare, which, for the first time, guaranteed the provision of health care for America's elderly. The promise of the federal government paying hospitals for the nation's growing elderly population forced institutions to abide by Title IV of the previous year's civil rights legislation. This prohibits discrimination based on race, color or national origin in programs that receive federal financial assistance, and authorities made clear their intent to enforce it for the Medicare program.

Besides the segregated health care system, the nursing profession also prohibited African American nurses from belonging to the American Nurses Association until 1951. Racial discrimination, however, persisted. Elizabeth Williams, a graduate of the program to train African American nurses at Mercy-Douglass Hospital in West Philadelphia, remembers being denied a job opportunity due to her skin color. After graduating from the program at Mercy-Douglass in 1954, Williams applied for work at the Harrisburg State Hospital in Harrisburg, Pennsylvania. The nursing director there refused to talk to Williams because of her race.

Well into the twenty-first century, obstacles continue to confront African American women who want to become nurses. These women compose only 5 percent of the nation's nurses—a disproportionate number compared to the percentage of America's overall population. Though she possessed extensive experience nursing, in the time immediately after the Second World War, Alma Bailey's career appeared over.

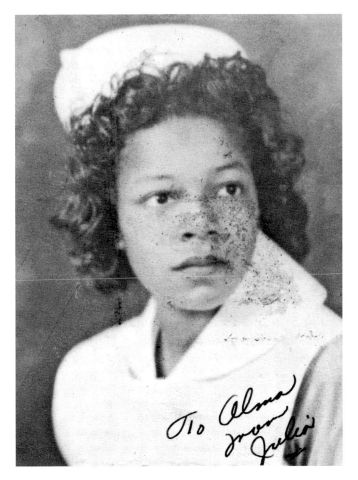

Tuskegee Sisterhood. *Philadelphia Chapter, Tuskegee Airmen.*

Then the unexpected occurred. One night, Bessie, the surgeon's maid admitted into the hospital near Alma Bailey's home in Kentucky, landed in the hospital postsurgery without any nurses to attend to her. The surgeon was worried about her safety (yet somehow not worried enough to stay himself). He put out a call for a black nurse to come to Bessie's aid, and Miss Bailey, who was at a party at the time, agreed to help. She received a ride to the hospital on a bicycle.

Without a uniform, adorned in one of her mother's dresses and wearing her brother's tennis shoes, Miss Bailey arrived at the hospital late in the evening and was asked to stay the night with Bessie, who was not expected to make it to the morning. Miss Bailey aspirated her wound, gave her a bath, talked to her and stood by her side. When the surgeon came in the next morning, the patient was so well recovered that he offered Miss Bailey a job at the hospital.

As Miss Bailey quickly learned at the hospital, she was "only supposed to take care of the white people." An aspect of segregated health care involved prioritizing the treatment of whites. African American patients often suffered from neglect. Miss Bailey worked to mitigate this unfair treatment.

She began work at seven o'clock in the morning and would take care of all the white patients until her shift ended at around seven o'clock each night. Miss Bailey then went downstairs and personally took care of the black patients on her own time. Oftentimes, she would go home at eleven o'clock in the morning, sometimes even later. Many of the black men had syphilis, but because she had experience in Tuskegee, she was successful in treating it. Miss Bailey ended up working at the hospital for almost ten years.

After about five years working at the hospital and living in Middleburg, her friend convinced Miss Bailey to move with her to California and "get themselves some boyfriends." Her friend (who was a trained dietician) and Miss Bailey decided not to tell anyone that they were nurses, and they got jobs at JJ Newberry Company. Miss Bailey lived in California for a few years until her sister got pregnant with her second set of twins, and her mother made her go back to Kentucky in a Model T Ford to take care of her sister.

Miss Bailey returned to her old job as a nurse for her previous employer and remained there for another five years before moving to Philadelphia in 1955 to look after her older cousin, whom she cared for until her death. Miss Bailey worked at the University of Pennsylvania hospital from 1955 to 1960. She then went to Children's Orphanage, where she was head nurse for two years.

In the early 1960s, Miss Bailey went to work for the Lankenau Hospital in Wynnewood, Pennsylvania, where she once again became involved in a controversial research study without her prior knowledge. This research sought to simulate certain space conditions that astronauts might face during missions. Miss Bailey explains that there were local Amish men who were conscientious objectors to the Vietnam War who came to the Lankenau Hospital to participate in the study.

These volunteers were subjected to extreme tests and conditions, including being asked to live in significantly cold conditions. Miss Bailey explains that test patients had to stay in a chilled hospital room for a month with just a blanket and T-shirt and shorts. Temperatures got down to 40 degrees. Other tests included 120- to 140-degree rooms for shorter periods. This contributed to the science that resulted in the United States' landing of Apollo 11 on the moon on July 20, 1969.

After a time at Lankenau Hospital, Miss Bailey returned to University Hospital because of the difficult commute from her home. At University Hospital, she once again was tasked with psychiatry patients. Miss Bailey enjoyed a fruitful end to her career, becoming heavily involved in her church community in addition to her work at the hospital, joining the Blessed Virgin Mary Church in Darby.

Since her retirement in 1987, Miss Bailey has continued to serve as a parishioner for her church and assists with parish food and nursing programs and is a proud member of the Greater Philadelphia chapter of Tuskegee Airmen. She serves as an extraordinary minister of the Eucharist and a member of the parish pastoral council.

As she is interviewed, Miss Bailey wears her Tuskegee Airmen baseball cap proudly. One notices her resolve and her strength. You cannot help but imagine a young soldier, perhaps distraught, perhaps wounded, sitting helplessly on a hospital bed, unsure of his future and his role in society. Miss Bailey comes to him and offers him some water. She speaks to him. She looks after him, and when he recovers and leaves the hospital, he does so knowing he is cared for.

Throughout her life, Miss Bailey illustrated that she not only was a talented and dedicated nurse but also a nurse who cared for the downtrodden and forgotten—those afflicted with disease or disability. She was consistently promoted and given large amounts of responsibility. And Miss Bailey worked assignments that others could not or would not—from psychiatric and syphilis-infected patients in Tuskegee, to late nights in a hospital basement in Kentucky, to astronaut test subjects in Pennsylvania.

When asked what she would like to tell younger generations today, she responded with disappointment that Tuskegee history was not taught more in her local schools and that young people too often forget the sacrifices made by many seventy years ago. She is happy that these are finally recognized by the media and the government. Miss Bailey also worries about today's violence, especially gun violence among young people. She "wants kids to stop shooting each other and get out and do something with their lives."

Miss Bailey downplays her own involvement at Tuskegee, instead choosing to focus on others. She tells of going to a local Tuskegee event where there were Tuskegee veteran pilots. An older white gentleman in a wheelchair

A moment of silence. *Library of Congress.*

approached them with tears rolling down his cheeks. He told them he was a bomber in World War II, and he came up to them and told them that they "saved his goddamn ass," thanking them profusely.

Of course, Alma Elizabeth Bailey and her colleagues—the nurses of Tuskegee—deserve the thanks of their colleagues and of their nation as well. They cared for those Airmen who came back broken. They did all that they could to enable them to become whole again while working themselves to overcome both the racism and sexism that they confronted before and after the war, often on their own.

BIBLIOGRAPHY

Adams, Michael C.C. *The Best War Ever: America and World War II.* Baltimore: Johns Hopkins Press, 1993.

Air Force Link. "General O. Benjamin Davis Jr." America's Air Force. Accessed July 13, 2019. http://www.af.mil.

Andrews, Michelle. "1965: The Year that Brought Civil Rights to the Hospitals." *Kaiser Health News.* Accessed August 5, 2019. https://khn.org.

Army War College (U.S.). *The Use of Negro Manpower in War.* Carlisle: Army War College, 1925.

Bielakowski, Alexander M., ed. *Ethnic and Racial Minorities in the U.S. Military: An Encyclopedia.* Santa Barbara, CA: ABC-CLIO, 2013.

Chidley, Mark. "Portraits of Valor: Iowa's Tuskegee Airman." 132nd Wing. Accessed July 29, 2019. https://www.132dwing.ang.

Clark, Alexis. "These Black Female Heroes Made Sure U.S. World War II Forces Got Their Mail." History. Accessed August 5, 2019. https://www.history.com.

Commonwealth of Pennsylvania. "History of Amendments." Pennsylvania Human Relations Commission. Accessed June 13, 2019. https://www.phrc.pa.gov.

Homan, Lynn M., and Thomas Reilly. *Black Knights: The Story of the Tuskegee Airmen.* Gretna, LA: Pelican Publishing, 2001.

Jan, Tracy. "Redlining Was Banned Fifty Years Ago, It Is Still Hurting Minorities Today." *Washington Post.* March 28, 2018. Accessed July 26, 2019. https://www.washingtonpost.com.

Jones, Ayana. "Mercy-Douglass School of Nursing Remembered, Honored." *Philadelphia Tribune,* April 28, 2014. Accessed July 31, 2019. https://www.phillytrib.com.

King, Martin L. "I Have a Dream." Speech presented at the March on Washington for Jobs and Freedom, Washington, D.C., August 1968. Accessed June 18, 2019. https://kinginstitute.stanford.edu.

Lyle, Amani. "Lonely Eagles Ceremony Recognizes Fallen Tuskegee Airmen." *U.S. Air Force* (news), August 17, 2009. Accessed August 6, 2019. https://www.af.mil.

Mullenbach, Cheryl. *Double Victory: How African American Women Broke Race and Gender Barriers to Help Win World War II.* Chicago: Chicago Review Press, 2013.

National Park Service. "Air(wo)man Discovered and Honored." U.S. Department of the Interior. Accessed July 29, 2019. https://www.nps.gov.
———. "And There Were Women." U.S. Department of the Interior. Accessed July 15, 2019. https://www.nps.gov.

Osur, Alan M. *Blacks in the Army Air Forces During World War II: The Problems of Race Relations.* Washington, D.C.: Office of Air Force History, United States Air Force, 1986.

Philadelphia Chapter of Tuskegee Airmen. Oral History Collection. Philadelphia, PA.

Rogers, Naomi. "Race and the Politics of Polio." *American Journal of Public Health* 97, no. 5 (2007): 784–95. Accessed August 3, 2019. doi:10.2105/ajph.2006.095406.

Scott, Lawrence P., and William M. Womack Sr. *Double V: The Civil Rights Struggle of the Tuskegee Airmen.* East Lansing: Michigan State University Press, 1992.

Siek, Stephanie. "Women of Tuskegee Supported Famed Black Pilots." CNN. Updated February 2, 2012. https://www.cnn.com.

Thompson, James. "Should I Sacrifice to Live 'Half-American'?" *Pittsburgh Courier.* January 31, 1942. Accessed June 18, 2019. http://blackquotidian.com.

Tuskegee Army Nurses Project. Accessed July 5, 2019. http://www.tuskegeearmynurses.info.

"A Woman's Perspective on Serving with the Tuskegee Airmen Support Personnel." *Caf Red Tail Squadron* (blog). October 13, 2014. Accessed August 2, 2019. https://www.redtail.org.

About the Authors

Robert J. Kodosky, PhD (Temple University), chairs the history department at West Chester University, where he teaches courses on American military and diplomatic history and advises the Student Veteran Group. He is the author of *Psychological Operations American Style: The Joint United States Public Affairs Office, Vietnam and Beyond* (Lexington, 2007).

Steven James Zaharick II ("Ladies First") did his undergraduate work in history at Bloomsburg University and is now pursuing his master of arts degree at West Chester University. A native of Pottsville, Pennsylvania, Steven is passionate about the preservation of local history.

Michael J. Weiss ("Trainers") studied history as both an undergraduate and graduate at West Chester University. He received the conference prize for best graduate paper at the 2019 Phi Alpha Theta regional meeting at Bloomsburg University for his work on the Katyn Massacre.

Michael Kowalski ("Bombers") is a high school social studies teacher from West Chester, Pennsylvania. He received his bachelor's degree in secondary education from Pennsylvania State University and a master of arts degree in history from West Chester University.

Jeffrey Markland ("Mechanics") is a native of West Chester, Pennsylvania and currently is working on his master of arts in history at West Chester University.

Brandon Ray Langston ("Escorts") is an undergraduate at West Chester University where he studies biology and history while regularly contributing opinion pieces and features to the university newspaper, the *Quad*.

Matthew Rothfuss ("Medical") works in the reference department at the Bethlehem Area Public Library in Bethlehem, Pennsylvania, where he coordinates educational events and teams on local history projects. Matthew obtained both his bachelor's degree and master of arts from West Chester University, specializing in modern U.S. history. Currently, he is pursuing a masters in library science from Clarion University and collaborating on an oral history project that focuses on the African American experience in Bethlehem.